HousePro Academy™ Presents:

Buy Your First Home

A Basic Step-by-Step Guide for First Time Home Buyers

by Regina P. Brown

www.HouseProAcademy.com

Buy Your First Home:

A Basic Step-by-Step Guide for First Time Home Buyers

FIRST EDITION, November 2012

Copyright © 2012 HousePro Academy

ISBN No. 978-1-62546-001-1 (paperback)

ISBN No. 978-1-62546-000-4 (hardcover)

ISBN No. 978-1-62546-002-8 (ebook)

Author: Brown, Regina P. 1967-

Illustrator: Dusgupta, Sudipta 1982-

Series: HousePro Academy Success Series

Publisher: Queen Bee Publisher Inc., Cheyenne WY

Library of Congress Cataloging-in-Publication Data

> Brown, Regina P.
> Buy Your First Home: A Basic Step-by-Step Guide for First Time Home Buyers
> Includes bibliographical references and index.
> ISBN No. 978-1-62546-000-4 (hardcover)
> ISBN No. 978-1-62546-001-1 (paperback)
> 1. Consumer finance 2. House buying 3. Real estate
> I. Title
> Library of Congress Control Number: 2012921746
> 643.12 – dc23

Summary: For renters who dream of becoming home owners, this comprehensive guide shows each phase of the home buying process in a simple step-by-step how-to manual that is easy to understand.

Topics: House buying, home, family, housing, self-help, reference guide, education, consumer finance, personal finance, real estate, economic training. Non-fiction.

PREFACE

Baseball. Chevy cars. Mom's apple pie. Does that make you think of "America"? Sometimes we take our basic virtues for granted. But people from all over the world cherish our values — they arrive here to get their slice of Americana and to pursue the American Dream.

What is the American Dream? It is the concept that we are in control of our own destiny. We can begin poor and create wealth through hard work. We can be entrepreneurs and invent, create, fulfill. We can worship God freely. We can each own our piece of land. Yes, the critical cornerstone of that American Dream is home ownership. It is the path to financial independence. It is a vital element of every family's legacy.

I strongly believe that every family should own their own home. My dream is to show millions of renters how to become homeowners. That's why I wrote this book as a guide that aspiring homeowners can follow. And you're reading it because you, too, share the dream of homeownership.

You may have some doubts about whether you can buy a home, or you may be uncertain about how the process works. You may be thinking, "The process is overwhelming. I don't even know where to begin. It's too complicated. Who's going to help me?"

Of course home buying takes some time, energy, and effort. But the freedom of home ownership is so rewarding, that I promise it will be worth your effort. What is more thrilling than to get the keys to your own home?

Yes, you can do it! All you need is a guide that you can follow, and a quality real estate professional to assist you.

Our book is outlined as a guide that you can easily understand. Just start with Step 1 and follow the 9 steps in this book. We will direct you each step of the way. We'll also show you how to hire a dedicated REALTOR® you can trust, so you will receive professional guidance and direction.

Let's get you the best home that your budget can afford. I know that you are going to read and follow these steps. So I dedicate this book to you! You have the courage to take action and make your dream of homeownership come true.

My "Home" Story

Before we bought our first home, I remember driving through the particular neighborhood I liked, seeing "For Sale" signs, and I kept thinking "Geez, those houses are too expensive, who would pay that much?" And every year the selling prices would get higher and higher. And I kept thinking, "I can't believe the values rose again... we should have bought last year!"

When we finally did purchase our home, I still felt the price was too high (you can see I'm the frugal type). But over the next few years, as the values kept rising, I was so relieved that we had the courage to purchase our home. It was the best financial and family decision we've ever made.

We had been hoping, wishing, and dreaming for years. Our apartment rent just kept going up and up. One day my dad called me and asked if we would like downpayment funds to buy a home. Of course I said "yes!" Dad's generosity was truly an answer to a prayer.

Did we ever jump for joy and praise God!!! Finally, our dream of homeownership was going to come true. A piece of American land was ours. My heart rejoiced. Now we wouldn't have to worry about moving unexpectedly or being at the whim of rent-raising landlord. We felt rooted and secure and at peace.

We were nervous because we didn't know what to expect. But our REALTOR® friend helped us navigate every phase of the home buying process, and we were so thankful to have her on our side. We bought a cute little condo with an FHA loan and soon moved in, with baby in tow. Of course, my caring mom came over to help me decorate make it all my own.

Our 1-year-old son loved the little yard — it was perfect for him to hit baseballs while his Grandma helped him keep score. And play baseball he did... every day! We enjoyed our little home and we were happy that we had finally taken the "leap" from renter to homeowner.

Over the years, we worked hard to improve the house to upgrade it from 1970's standards to reflect modern style and convenience. The personal touches were truly labors of love. Eventually our daughter was born, and shortly thereafter we moved up to a larger home to accommodate our growing family.

Our home is so much more than simply a house. A **house** is a building but **home** is where we live. Our home is our sanctuary, our refuge from the outside world. It's our retreat from the barrage of work and school and traffic and stress. Home is a place where our family loves and grows and flourishes. Our home holds our past memories of good times we enjoyed together. The stability of being grounded at home gives us the confidence to dream and hope for the future, and the jumping-off point from which to pursue our ambitions and realize our aspirations.

I hope that you, too, will gather the courage to take action and buy your first home. Remember that success doesn't happen overnight, but if you take one step towards your goal every day, you **will** realize your home ownership dream come true!

Acknowledgements

Thank you to those who paved the road for me. Elaine Swann, what an inspiration as a classy business lady! I figured that if you wrote a book, I could do it too. So I just followed in your footsteps. Keeping shining the light on the path ahead!

I would like to acknowledge and thank: Glenna Bloemen, my heaven-sent angel who collected 45 years of dreaming and took action to make my book real and tangible and touchable; Steve Dusgupta the talented artist who drew the charming illustrations and breathed new life into the story; My editor, Ashley Ratcliff, who imparted professionalism; and I must acknowledge my consultant and friend, Miriam Fajardo, a sharp lady who can tackle any project! I'm glad that you are all on my team.

To my teachers, instructors, and professors who recognized my talents. Thank you for attempting to mold me and nurture my skills, regardless of my stubborn resistance. You knew I was a born author. You knew I had it in me. I'm sure I was a source of endless frustration because I (seemingly) didn't embrace my natural talents. The seeds you sowed in my life have finally come to fruition. I hope that my success gives you the motivation to keep teaching and molding lives, even when you may not see the immediate outcome.

To my fellow employees at my "real job" experience and to the entrepreneurs with whom I honed my business skills – I learned something every day. Sometimes what TO DO and sometimes what NOT to do. Most importantly, you helped me discover my passion and gave me the impetus to pursue it.

To my team of faithful business associates: I value your friendship. I appreciate your loyalty and dedication. You keep me motivated to push forward each day! Thank you for entrusting me with the opportunity to lead, guide, and influence your career. I hope to sow good seeds into your life, as were sown into mine.

To the book authors in whose steps I have followed, thank you for paving the road before me. To both my business colleagues and my competitors: you challenged me and drove me to succeed.

To all those who guided, supported, and encouraged me gently (and sometimes bluntly). So many people cared enough to sow good seeds into my life, helping me grow and blossom... thank you! Your care and concern is much appreciated.

Dedication

Thanks to God my Creator, who took the effort to divinely design me with His touch and created me strong and smart and special. Lord, I am blessed and thrilled and humbled that You granted me such a unique and authentic stamp of individuality.

I thank everyone who invested in me and my life and my family. First and foremost, I thank my Mom who is always my #1 fan. Mom, you sacrificed yourself for your children. I pray you earn rich dividends on your investment! Dad and Mom, you always believed in me, even though at times you did not understand me. I know I can keep fighting because you're in my corner.

Growing up we had a "no frills" lifestyle. I observed you, my parents, working hard, managing your limited finances well, and investing prudently for the future. You may not have understood my ambition and passion and vision. But you always provided a great example. I appreciate your principles of integrity and hard work; they comprise the solid foundation upon which I have built my life.

This Book is Dedicated:

To my children, Carl Bruce Kenton and Carlynn Katrina Estelle, who are my special Gifts from God. He gave me YOU at a time in my life when I needed you most. You bring me so much joy and your happiness is my greatest life achievement. I'm so very proud of you both. I wince when I hear your criticisms but they are always a strong reality check that keeps me grounded, and your wit makes me laugh at myself. And I'm proud of my newest son, Jordan Lawrence Frye who is divinely tasked with the challenging project of taking care of my baby girl.

To my husband who pushed me into a real estate career, which I have come to relish. I am encouraged by your tenacity and inspired by your boldness. Truly, I appreciate your sacrifices and support to help me keep my "book" dream alive.

To my House of Prayer family, who sustained me and showed me how to stand on Jesus the Rock, when I had nothing left to stand on. To my Shiloh family who adopted me at a time in my life when I needed direction.

To my sister Serina Faye whose "big sister admiration" for me, gave me the confidence to embrace my role as a leader. You turned out to be a terrific lady, in spite of my bossiness. I love you. Keep being a great Mommy for your family!

To my grandparents -- I didn't fully appreciate your resourcefulness until you were gone. Grandma Katy, Grandma Sue, and Grandpa Wimpy, a small piece of you continues on inside me. I'm thankful for the deposits/investments you made in my life. I miss your words of wisdom. And oh how I wish I would have spent more time learning your life experiences and sharing our family heritage. Because your legacy is my heritage.

To the reader... for purchasing and reading my book... thank you! I am so very grateful to you for your support and friendship. Come along and continue the journey with me. We've only just started! ☺ And so much more to come...

CONTENTS

INTRODUCTION 13

Purpose.. 14

Why Buy a Home? 14

HOMEBUYER STEPS 17

Renting Versus Owning... 18

Who Are First Home Buyers? 19

What's Holding You Back? 24

Overview 25

How Do I Select a REALTOR®? 27

STEP 1: Prepare For Home Ownership 31

1. Write Down Financial Goals 32

2. Prepare Your Monthly Budget.. 33

3. Upgrade Your Credit Score 36

4. Eliminate Consumer Debt 38

5. Save Money 41

6. Enroll in Home Buying Course 44

7. Change Your Mindset.. 45

STEP 2: Get Ready to Shop for Houses 47

1. Research Neighborhoods.. 48

2. Interview Lenders 50

3. Give Docs to Lender.. 53

4. Get Qualified... 55

5. Calculate Monthly Payment 56

6. Pre-Approval Letter 58

7. Sign Buyer/Broker Representation Agreement 59

8. Include Decision-Makers 60

9. New Listings on Market 61

10. Drive by Selected Houses 62

11. Property Types 62

STEP 3: Find A House **71**

1. Drive by Houses.. 72
2. Select Houses to View 74
3. Bring Your Checkbook 75
4. View Inside of Homes 76
5. Take Notes 79
6. Can You Take Photos? 80
7. Number Your Favorites 81
8. Narrow to One House 83

STEP 4: Write Your Offer **85**

1. Go Back to the Office... 85
2. Discuss the Price and Terms of the Offer................................ 86
3. Call the Listing Agent 88
4. View Neighborhood Comps 89
5. Write an Offer 91
6. Prepare for Inspection and Negotiate the Home Warranty 93
7. Sign the Purchase Offer 96

STEP 5: Purchase Contract **99**

1. Major Items in Purchase Contract 99
2. Major Closing Costs for Buyers 103
3. Notes 106

STEP 6: Negotiations.. **107**

1. Negotiations.. 108
2. Counter Offer 110
3. Negotiating Process 110
4. Continue Shopping 111
5. Further Negotiations 112
6. Document Review? 113
7. Pack for Your Move... 114
8. Keep a Backup Plan 115

STEP 7: Escrow Process 117

1. Open Escrow 118
2. Home Inspection and Reports..119
3. Order Appraisal 122
4. Sign Disclosures 123
5. Review Title Report 124
6. Get Homeowners Insurance 126
7. Final Loan Approval 128
8. Plan Your Moving Date 129

STEP 8: Closing Escrow 131

1. Find Neighborhood Services..131
2. Do Not Buy New Furniture!...133
3. Inspect the House 133
4. Review Closing Docs...135
5. Review Loan Docs...135
6. Sign Loan Docs 136
7. Pay Your Closing Costs 137
8. Wire Loan Funds 138
9. Get Utilities Connected...139
10. Pick Up Your Keys!..140

STEP 9: Your New Home...141

1. Congratulations! 141
2. Call the Movers 142
3. Appreciate Your Service Providers 143
4. Give Thanks 144
5. Take Care of the House...145
6. Home Warranty 147
7. Pay Your Mortgage 148
8. Review Your Budget 150
9. Protect Your Assets 152

CONCLUSION 157

Questions? 158
Forms and Samples 158

Resources 159

Action Steps 160

APPENDIX 161

Glossary 163

Acronyms 177

Bibliography 181

Index 183

FORMS 189

Wish List 191

Budget Sample 193

Loan Comparison 197

Rent vs. Own Calculation 199

Agent Interview 201

House Comparison Form 203

Vendors on Your Team 207

Offer Checklist 209

ABOUT US 211

About HousePro Academy 213

Author Biography 215

INTRODUCTION

Hello! Thank you for joining us here at HousePro Academy. Our topic is "Buy Your First Home: The Home Buyer Basics" and we are going to show you how to go through each step to find and purchase your family's dream home.

After completing this book, you will be prepared to get qualified and buy your own home with the help from your team of professionals, including your REALTOR® and mortgage lender. If your dream is go from renter to homeowner, you are in the right place. We will show you exactly how to get there!

> *"Owning property in these old United States takes on a special meaning seen nowhere else in the world. The United States was built on ownership of property. Home ownership yields certain rights and privileges that cannot be obtained simply by paying someone else rent money to let you live somewhere for a while. A person's home is a castle. A homestead. You own it."* p.xxii (Reed, 2008)

Renting Vs. Home Ownership

Now, let's talk about paying rent to your landlord. If you are a renter, did you know that you are already paying a mortgage? It is just not YOUR mortgage. When you pay your rent each month, you are paying for the landlord's mortgage, taxes, and insurance payment. You are helping your landlord to buy his house. You make all the payments. After 30 years, the mortgage is paid off. He owns the house free and clear, and yet you will continue paying rent for the rest of your life. Now, that's enough motivation to make you want to buy your own home, isn't it?

What caused you to start thinking seriously about home ownership? Maybe it was a major life event, such as graduating from college, getting married, or having a baby. Maybe you are intrigued because of the low prices and interest rates today. Whatever your reason is, we are glad you are here. Today you are taking the first step toward creating your future. Are you ready? Let's get started!

Purpose

This guide book is designed for anyone who is a renter and wants to own their own home, including:

- Newly married couples
- Families with children
- College graduates
- Military personnel relocating
- Singles with a "solo" household
- Extended generation families

Our book is for simply **any American** who wants to own their own home. Even if you are a family of just one person, you too can be a homeowner.

> *"The average renter in the United States has less than $5,000 in wealth. The average homeowner has nearly $200,000, which is 40 times as much wealth as a renter... Most of their wealth is their home and they built up this wealth by owning a home instead of renting one. The easiest way to become wealthy is to become a homeowner. It really is as simple as that." p.10 (Smith, 2008)*

Why Buy a Home?

Why should you buy your own home? The most common reasons are listed here, but I am sure you already have your own reasons. Some renters live in an apartment with no yard, and they desire to move to a single-family residence with a yard for the kids to play in. Instead of continuing to rent, they decide to buy a home.

Maybe you are living with your parents and it's time for you to own your own home. Perhaps your rental situation is unstable because the landlord's mortgage loan is in foreclosure. Or your family is expecting a baby and you need room to expand.

Some folks simply say, *"I want to have something tangible to show for my money."* That is another way of saying that you work hard, so you want to invest your money into something that you can really touch, feel, and see, which helps you recognize the value of your efforts.

Cheaper Than Rent

In today's real estate market, it is cheaper to own a home than to rent in 98 of the top 100 metro areas of the United States, according to a recent article published by The Huffington Post (Kavoussi, 2012). That is truly astounding! In most places in America, a mortgage housing payment often costs the same or less than rent. While home prices won't stay this low forever, any time is a great time to buy if it makes financial sense for your family's budget.

> *"As the cost of living goes up, the cost of rent goes right up with it. If you use a fixed-rate mortgage to buy a home, however, your principal and interest payments stay the same for as long as you live in the home. The longer you stay there, the more pronounced this benefit."*
> p.4 (Conner, 2010)

Family Stability

The second reason is family stability. You know you and your family will be living in one place for a long time. If you have children in school, you know they are not going to have to change schools just because your landlord gave you a notice to move. Children thrive when they know they have a stable home to come back to every day.

Once you get to know your neighbors, you and your family will feel safe in the community. In a great community, kids play together and neighbors look out for each other. A good neighborhood offers a sense of security to residents.

Tax Benefits

The third reason is the tax benefit of being able to write off your mortgage interest, property taxes, and other costs on your annual income taxes. By itemizing their tax deductions, homeowners find that they save money because they owe less federal and state taxes. That is much different from renting and it is a big reason why many renters decide to buy a home.

> *"For decades, estate planning has been significantly impacted by the federal transfer tax system; namely, estate tax, gift tax, and the generation-skipping transfer tax."* p.3 (Moy, 2003)

Anticipated Appreciation

Another reason is anticipated appreciation. This is why many homeowners invest in a house and think of it as an investment. Although, I would caution you NOT to buy a house solely for future appreciation, because the house may depreciate in the short term, depending on the market.

However, studies have shown that during the long term, homeowners will often realize an appreciation rate of about 5% per year. That is why we talk about buying and owning for the long term. Renters do not build wealth. Home owners do.

> *"It is best to plan on living in your home for at least 3-5 years before selling. This means that having a stable job situation is paramount... The ideal situation is for you to be financially stable, have a stable career, and have a desire to stay in one place for the near future."*
> (Peebles, 2012)

In this book, we advise you to think long-term when you purchase your home and plan to stay in the home at least 5-10 years. Although the best strategy is to stay longer so you can earn more equity, we realize that families often have to relocate due to job transfers, wanting to be closer to family, and other reasons. But the longer you can stay, the more equity you will build.

Future Retirement

Another great reason to own your home is future retirement. After you pay off your mortgage, you will own your home free and clear without any monthly mortgage payments. All you will have to pay are your taxes and insurance each year, and perhaps homeowner dues, if you live in a homeowners association (HOA) community. Therefore, with your mortgage payment gone, your overhead is greatly reduced and you can afford to retire. That is a great future to look forward to!

Asset Investment

Many families start with home ownership as the foundation of their wealth strategy. As you build your financial portfolio, buying your first home can be a vital stepping-stone to wealth management. As you pay down your mortgage loan balance, you gain equity.

> *"Your home is your castle, an immense source of pride where you can live securely and comfortably. But your home is also a very important investment, probably the most important investment you will ever make." (Smith, 2008) p.5*

Although we do not advise you to purchase your family's home as a way to get rich, we do recognize that many homeowners will eventually "move up" to a larger home for their family. When they do, they often keep their first house as a rental property. They hope to receive a small income from the cash flow each month, and then pay off the mortgage and receive a larger cash flow. The rental income helps supplement their fixed budget during retirement years.

It Is All Yours!

The main reason to buy a home is that it is all yours! You can paint it. You can hang pictures. You can improve it your way. You can install new appliances. You can renovate with new carpets or hardwood floors. You can add a patio and barbecue in the back yard. Go ahead and decorate, remodel, or add on an extra room for your expanding family – it's all yours.

Renters have many rules and restrictions to follow. Maybe you want to have a pet but your landlord says "no". Perhaps your ailing grandmother wants to come live with you so you can take care of her at home. But as a homeowner, there are no landlord restrictions limiting pets or people in your home. The children can get a puppy if they want to. Your family members can move in and you do not need permission from a landlord. Also, when you are a homeowner, there is no landlord to give you a notice to move out. You don't have to move unless YOU want to. Your home is all yours to enjoy for many future generations.

HOMEBUYER STEPS

This guide book teaches you the nine steps to go from renter to homeowner.

9 Steps to Your New Home!

STEP 9: Your New Home

STEP 8: Closing Escrow

STEP 7: Escrow Process

STEP 6: Negotiations

STEP 5: Purchase Contract

STEP 4: Write your Offer

STEP 3: House Shopping

STEP 2: Get Ready to Shop for Houses

STEP 1: Prepare For Home Ownership

The first step is to **prepare for home ownership**. We are going to show you exactly what you need to do to become a qualified, serious, motivated buyer. We will show you how to get your credit ready and secure a good mortgage loan.

The second step is **getting ready to shop for houses** and find the type of neighborhood you want to live in.

Step three is to **shop for a house**. We are going to show you how to get daily email alerts of new homes listed for sale from your REALTOR®.

The fourth step is to **make your purchase offer** and get the price and terms that are best for you.

Step five covers the **items in your offer and purchase contract**. We are going to discuss California specifically, but most states have a similar process.

The sixth step is the **negotiation** phase and arriving at the mutual price and terms that will suit all parties; including appliances that are included with the sale, what items the sellers will repair, and what day you will be closing.

Step seven is what to expect **during escrow** including the inspection process, escrow documents, disclosures, your mortgage loan, and closing escrow.

Congratulations! The eighth step is **closing escrow** and taking possession of your new home.

Step nine is **enjoying your home** after you purchase your new house. This also details how to keep your lovely home, in good condition, and how to protect your assets for your future generations.

Renting Versus Owning

Now let's discuss the difference between renting and owning a home. Some of it has to do with our mentality; in other words, the way that you and I think about things, and how we view them.

When you are a renter, you are not responsible for many things. When something around the house breaks, you just call your landlord and he or she gets it fixed. Your landlord is responsible for paying all the bills on the house, including mortgage, taxes, and insurance. It is easy to sit back and let the landlord do everything.

When you are a homeowner, YOU take on the responsibility of making sure the mortgage, taxes, and insurance are paid; and YOU also have to take care of repairs. Therefore, you can see it is a different mentality. It is a mindset of being responsible for something because YOU own it.

Renters do not think long-term about security, stability, assets for their children, and future legacy. However, homeowners do. That is what we will focus on in this course.

Rent Only Goes Up; a Fixed-Rate Mortgage Loan Stays the Same

The main difference between renting and owning is that rent only goes up. In fact, have you ever heard of a landlord lowering your rent? No, that never happens. The landlord's goal is to raise the rent over a process of years. When you are a renter, your rent is only going to go up every year, but if you are a homeowner with a fixed-rate mortgage loan, as we advise, your payment never goes up. It stays the same until the loan is paid.

Rent Is Never Paid Off; But a Mortgage Can Be Paid Off

Even better, once you pay off your mortgage, you own your home "free and clear". So whether you have a 15-year, 20-year, or 30-year loan, you will eventually pay it off and then you would not have any more loan payments at all! Whereas if you are a renter, your rent will never be paid off and you will continue being a renter the rest of your life.

Renters Must Move with Short Notice

If you are a renter, the landlord can give you a 30 or 60 days' notice to vacate. Then you would have to move out, uproot your family, and scramble to look for another neighborhood to move to, while you try to keep your kids in the same schools. If you own your home, you know that you are not going to be moving unless YOU choose to.

Renters Cannot Change or Remodel the Apartment

If you are a renter, the landlord probably has many rules you have to follow. For example, you cannot paint your daughter's bedroom wall her favorite color purple; you cannot put up your family photos on the walls because of the nails; you cannot remove the carpet and put in hardwood flooring just because it is better for your son's allergies. Maybe your wife is tired of cooking dinner on the old, worn-out stove and wants a newer, better, model — but the landlord isn't going to pay for that.

However, when YOU own the house, you have the opportunity to remodel it, fix it up, paint, and personalize it the way you and your family desire.

Rent Versus Buy Calculation

There is also an important calculation that you should do when deciding if you should continue renting or buy a house. That is called a *Rent versus Buy calculation*, and a blank form has been included in the Appendix of this book. Visit the Ginnie Mae website for some great online calculators at *www.GinnieMae.gov/ypth* including buy versus rent estimate, affordability calculator, and loan estimator calculator.

Who Are First Home Buyers?

First time home buyers are young and old, married and single, employees and business owners. They come from all cultures and nationalities. Below are some statistics from the National Association of Realtors® report entitled "Profile of Home Buyers and Sellers 2011" published 2011 in Washington DC by National Association of Realtors®. (National Association of Realtors®, 2012)

Household Composition

This chart shows that 54% of families were married couples, but nearly half of households were comprised of singles and unmarried couples. You don't have to be married with a 2-income family to buy your first home. 33% of first home buyers were singles!

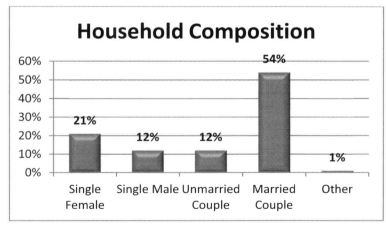

Household Composition -First Home Buyers 1

Age of First Home Buyers

Most first home buyers were between the age of 25 to 34 years old, but buyers spanned the range from 18 years old to 75 years old. In other words, it's never too early, nor too late, to become a home owner!

Annual Household Income

The household annual income also spanned a large range, with 5% of first home buyers earning a household income of less than $25,000. Most household earned between $25,000 and $75,000, but some first home buyers had income over $200,000 per year.

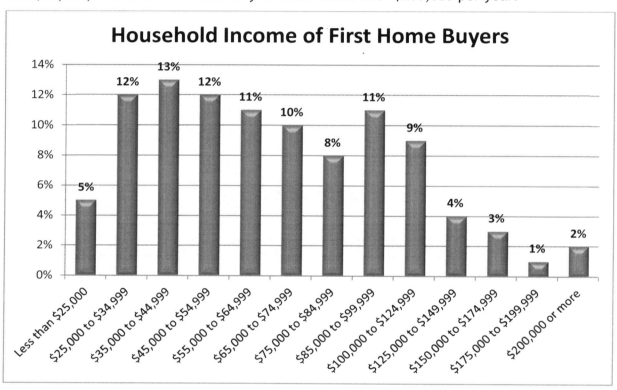

Household Income of First Home Buyers 2

Primary Reasons That Home Buyers Purchased A Home

First home buyers were driven by many forces, both internal and external. Their reasons for purchase included:

- Desire to own a home of my own
- Desire for larger home
- Job-related relocation or move
- Change in family situation
- Affordability of homes
- Desire to be closer to family/friends/relatives
- Desire for a home in a better area
- Retirement
- Desire for smaller home
- Desire to be closer to job/school/transit
- Establish household
- Greater number of homes on the market for sale/better choice

- Financial security
- Desire for a newly built or custom-built home
- Purchased home for family member or relative
- Tax benefits

Type of Home Purchased

First home buyers purchased all types of homes, but 73% bought the most popular type, single family residences (SFR). Please refer to the end of Step 2 for a complete discussion of the differences between each type of home building.

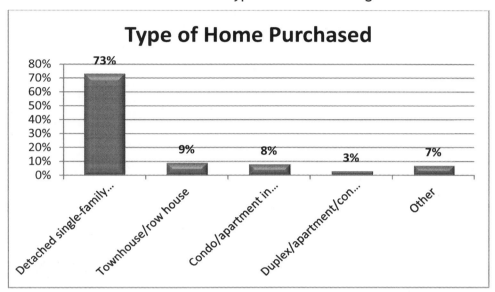

Type of Home Purchased 3

Location of Home Purchased

46% of first home buyers purchased their new home in a suburb or subdivision while 26% bought in an urban area or central city. The remaining home buyers bought houses in small towns, rural areas, and resort or recreation areas.

Sacrifices Made to Purchase Home

Many home buyers made financial sacrifices to be able to purchase their home. Note that 42% made NO sacrifices at all! The sacrifices were listed as:

- Cut spending on luxury items or non-essential items
- Cut spending on entertainment
- Cut spending on clothes
- Canceled vacation plans
- Sold a vehicle or decided not to purchase a vehicle
- Earned extra income through a second job

Price of Home Purchased

You can see that home prices varied greatly. The prices of the homes purchased ranged from less than $75,000 to over $500,000. Values are so different geographically in the U.S., from the highs of New York and California to the lows of the Midwest and Great Plains areas. Affordability rates depend on the local salary levels that also vary by region, so wherever you live, you can secure a great home that fits your income.

Price of Home Purchased 4

Sources of Downpayment

First home buyers were resourceful in gathering downpayment funds from many different sources, including:

- Savings
- Proceeds from sale of primary residence
- Gift from relative or friend
- Sale of stocks or bonds
- 401k/pension fund including a loan
- Inheritance
- Loan from relative or friend
- Individual Retirement Account (IRA)
- Equity from primary residence buyer continued to own
- Loan or financial assistance from source other than employer
- Proceeds from sale of real estate other than primary residence
- Loan from financial institution other than a mortgage
- Loan or financial assistance through employer

Number of Years Expected to Live in Home

Most first home buyers expect to live in their new house for at least 8 years, with 24% planning to live in their home for 16 or more years. Talk about a long-term investment!

We always advise you to hold your property for the long-term so you'll have the opportunity to earn equity. With a long-term investment of 10 or more years, you won't be affected by short-term swings in the real estate market.

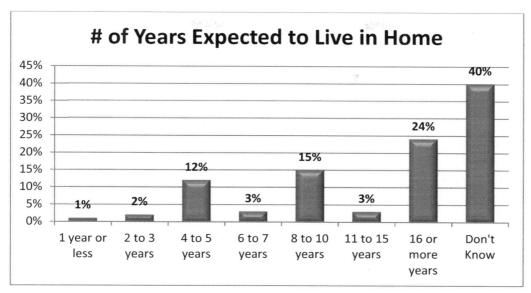

# of Years Expected to Live in Home 5

Type of Loan / Type of Mortgage

Most first home buyers (54%) obtained an FHA loan, and almost one third (30%) obtained a conventional loan. The balance of the buyers obtained VA or other types of loan. And 94% of buyers were smart enough to obtain a fixed-rate mortgage loan.

Most Difficult Steps of Home Buying Process

Almost all first home buyers hired an experienced real estate agent to help them overcome the challenges in the process. Some did not find any steps difficult at all. Others identified the following difficult steps:

- Finding the right property
- Paperwork
- Understanding the process and steps
- Getting a mortgage
- Saving for the down payment
- Appraisal of the property

Homeownership as a Good Financial Investment

The great majority (81%) of first home buyers thought that buying a home was a good financial investment, with only 14% undecided. Just think how excited those home owners will be when they have earned equity after a few years!

Characteristics of Home Compromised

We know that we can't always get our entire wish list of features "granted" in a first home purchase. Most home buyers had to compromise on some features. But surprisingly, 32% of first home buyers did NOT have to compromise at all! Most common "wish list" features compromised were:

- Price of home
- Condition of home
- Size of home
- Style of home
- Distance from job
- Lot size

- Distance from friends or family
- Quality of the neighborhood
- Quality of the schools
- Distance from school

Conclusion

With all of these figures and facts from the National Association of Realtors® report, we see that almost anyone can become a homeowner. Regardless of regional home values and regardless of income level, millions of people are buying homes every year in the U.S. If others can do it, you can too!

What's Holding You Back?

Sometimes I hear objections from renters who are hesitant to buy a home now. They are worried that the prices will go down in the future. They want to buy only at the "bottom" of the real estate market. They want to get the best value – doesn't everyone! But also they don't want to have their property depreciate after they purchase it.

Make the commitment! Think about WHY you want to become a homeowner. Then stick to your goal by taking action. "On a day-to-day basis, until you're in your new home, you must make a...commitment to move forward on your plan and inch closer to homeownership," says Tara-Nicholle Nelson on page 23 of her book, "The Savvy Woman's Homebuying Handbook." (Tara-Nicholle Nelson, 2006) She emphasizes the importance of overcoming fear and other obstacles, and shows how to move forward with confidence.

Don't Fret About Depreciation

My advice is: Don't worry about tomorrow's value going up or down. The main thing is that you can afford to pay the mortgage every month. If you have a low-rate fixed mortgage, you are comfortable with the amount, and you know that you will be able to continue making the payments over the long term, then why does it matter if the value goes down slightly? Studies show that real estate values appreciate by an average of 5% per year over a long period of time (10 or 15 years).

No matter what the "experts" say, NOBODY has a crystal ball and NO ONE knows when the market is truly at the bottom. The only way you know is when it starts going back up again. Then you can look at the previous values and say, 'yes, it was at the bottom'. But by then it's too late, as the values are already rising. Which also means there are many buyers and it will be more difficult to purchase because of the competition.

> *"Fact is, nobody knows where the bottom of the market is. We'll only know after it...is on the way back up... Waiting often doesn't pay. Buyer opportunities have never been better." (Buffini, 2008)*

If you purchase now, and start building equity and appreciation, you will be thankful that you got started. "I have heard both sides of the argument on how beneficial home ownership is financially. As a homeowner you have tax deductions on the interest on your loan, property tax deductions. Yes, you do have to come up with monies up front, and then there are maintenance costs. But in the end, we all need a place to live. Why not have something that belongs to you." (blog comment from Cecilia Kleiner, KleinerProperties.com)

You'll Find the Right House – Don't Worry!

Sometimes prospective home buyers are worried that they may not be able to find just the right house for them. Maybe it seems there are so many houses available, that searching for the "right house" could be overwhelming. Maybe the real estate market is experiencing a "lack of inventory" and there's a shortage of homes, so they don't want to have to compete with other buyers for their dream home.

> *"There are 65 million homes in this country and in any year about 7 million, or 10 percent, are for sale. These run the gamut from brand-new houses to properties more than 100 years old. They include single-family homes, condos, and co-ops." p.1 (Irwin, 2002)*

The bottom line is that at any given time, people move. Sometimes people move for happy reasons, like a job transfer, expanding their family, or moving up to a larger house. Other times, people must move due to death, divorce, or disability. No matter what the market is like, there are always houses available for sale in the neighborhood that's right for you. And your real estate agent will help you compete and win your new home for you.

Overview

Owning my home represents freedom to me. I am in control of my home, my possessions, and my financial future. I can make my own decisions about how to improve my home the way I want to. I don't have to move unless I choose to. I don't have to worry about a nosy landlord.

When I come home from work every day, I look around and I am happy that my home suits my family and me. I work hard and I want something tangible to show for my hard work. It makes going to work — worthwhile. And best of all, I know my children will always have something of their own and a place to call "home". That's what I call, "real freedom".

These days it seems like every news channel is talking about the low prices of real estate, the opportunity for home ownership, and how much cheaper it is to buy a home than to rent. Perhaps you have been seriously considering that for yourself and your family.

Thinking about Buying?

Are you thinking about buying a home in the future? With the current buyer's market, home values are now more affordable than ever.

So, you've been thinking about finally moving out of that apartment and buying your very first home. Every time you drive by the house on the corner, you get excited thinking that JUST MAYBE it is the house for you. You can see yourself driving into the garage, unloading your groceries in that nice, big kitchen and barbecuing on your new grill in the back yard.

You pick up your phone and call the real estate agent whose smiling photo is on the sign in the yard. You tell her you want to see the inside of the house — and instead, she asks if you are pre-qualified!

Buying is a Process!

Okay, so now you know there is a process for buyers and it is not instant. It is not as simple as just viewing a home and then buying it and moving in. It is your dream to own a house, but it can be overwhelming — where do you start? For renters who want to buy a home, this step-by-step guide can prepare you.

Hire a REALTOR®

Don't worry! Your trusted REALTOR® will be there to help you walk through every step of the process. That is why you need to hire a real REALTOR®; a real estate consultant who will be your buyer's agent and can guide you through each phase. Since this is your first time buying a home, your REALTOR® will represent you professionally and negotiate on your behalf.

It is so important to have that experience and knowledge in your corner and to have a professional going to bat for you. Don't cut corners by trying to do it all yourself.

The best part about hiring a Buyer's Agent to represent you is that you do not have to pay your agent any money! That is right, in most parts of the United States, the seller pays the agent's compensation.

By the way, I use the term REALTOR® because I strongly recommend that you hire a real estate agent who is a member of the National Association of REALTORS® (NAR). Why? They are highly regarded professionals who follow a strict code of ethics.

Financing Options are Available

This is the best time to buy! Lenders are eager to lend money and there are more options available to you today than ever before. Finding a good mortgage loan, qualifying, and financing your purchase are major parts of buying a home.

You need to know that there are many, many options available to you. There is financing available for down payment assistance, closing costs, the loan type, and interest rate. In fact, some first-time homebuyers qualify for a 100% loan and, in addition, there are grants available from many sources, down payment assistance; and, loans that include repairs and improvements.

Married Couples must Decide Together

You need to know that married couples must decide together. If you are married, both you and your husband or wife must participate in the process and sign the documents together. That means you both must agree on the type of house you want, shop for the house together, and make the decisions together.

It means that you are both legally responsible for paying the mortgage loan and taking care of the house. Most likely, both of your names will be on the mortgage loan and you will be taking title together.

Even if the husband or the wife is purchasing a home separately, the other spouse still must sign off the paperwork, because of community property laws in most states. Therefore, you both must be involved in the process and you will need to make your decision together.

If you are buying the house with someone else, for example, your sister or brother is helping you qualify for the loan, then you all are equally responsible. If your parents are giving you money for the down payment, then they probably will want to help you select the best house possible, so get them involved in the process early.

Homeownership is a Different Mentality from Renting

Okay, now it is time to put on our homeowner hat. We are going to switch our mentality from being a renter to being a homeowner. A renter relies on the landlord to pay all the bills on the property and to maintain the exterior and the structural aspects of the home.

When you are a renter, you expect others to take care of things for you. You simply have to pay your rent and the landlord pays the mortgage, the taxes, and the insurance. If anything breaks, your landlord has to fix it. The renter is passive and does not have to take much responsibility.

However, once you become a homeowner, you will assume the responsibilities for the costs and the maintenance. You are elevating yourself to a new level of maturity and responsibility. In return, your rewards are immeasurable. You get to paint, remodel, and decorate your home the way YOU want to. You get to make the decisions and you are in control of your family's future. You are now in the driver's seat!

You Must Take ACTION

Education and knowledge are great, but they are worthless if you do not take action. I have seen some prospective homebuyers who were afraid to take that next step to home ownership. Maybe they were scared to step out of their comfort zone, or maybe they did not think they would qualify. We are going to equip you with the tools and resources you need to succeed, and there is no excuse NOT to follow your dream of homeownership.

Start by taking the first step today by reading this guide and taking notes. Then make an action list for you and your family to move on to the next step. The most important thing is to DO SOMETHING every day to help you reach your goal. Take action today and be persistent until your dreams come true. I promise that it will be fun and exciting, too!

How Do I Select a REALTOR®?

We have talked a lot about your Realtor® who will help guide you through the entire home buying process. You know how critical it is to select the right professional to work with you, but just how do you find and hire the right person? Let's discuss that now.

Where Do I Find a REALTOR®?

How do you find a great REALTOR®? Just like when you select a mortgage lender, you can ask your friends and family, co-workers and neighbors, who they recommend. Look around your neighborhood, and see which real estate agent has the most houses for sale and observe which REALTORS® are holding open houses.

Research the top 5 agents by reviewing their online resumes at LinkedIn. It is a great place to start, and you should read their blogs to find out how much they know. For example, *ActiveRain* is an online source for top real estate agents who write blogs and articles.

Communication Style

What is your communication style? It is important to select a Realtor® who operates with the same communication style as you do. Are you a young person who prefers to text message or Skype your friends rather than call them on the phone? Would you prefer to meet up on Facebook instead of in person? Are you from the boomer generation and e-mail is best for you? Do you prefer written letters and cards, along with a personal handshake when you meet someone in person? You will find this step critical as you go through the process because you need to communicate with your agent frequently.

Along with the communication style, you need to know how responsive your agent will be in communicating with you. Will she contact you on a regular basis throughout the transaction? Does he return your phone calls and answer your emails promptly? Is she available when you need her? Of course, you cannot expect your agent to be available 24/7, but he should be available to assist you during regular business hours.

If you speak another language besides English, perhaps you would feel more comfortable working with an agent who speaks that language, too. Although that should not be the primary criteria for selecting an agent, it may help you feel more comfortable in communicating.

Experience, Knowledge, and Training

You will want to hire a REALTOR® who has experience working with first-time buyers. You need someone who is specially trained on affordable loans and down payment assistance programs, and someone who has the knowledge because he or she has successfully helped many homebuyers to purchase their homes. When interviewing, ask how many continuing education and professional development classes they attend regularly.

One way to find out if your real estate agent is knowledgeable is to look at her business card and web site. You may find out that he is certified in a certain area of real estate, or has earned a designation. Two designations of particular importance to buyers are the Graduate REALTOR® Institute (GRI) and the accredited buyer's representative (ABR). Agents with those designations have gone through special training to learn how to help a buyer like you.

Team Support and Vendors

In the real estate business, it is critical to be supported by a team of top professionals, and your REALTOR® already works with many partner vendors. We are talking about service providers you can count on to do a great job. People who can be trusted, are experienced, and have a superior record of serving buyers.

A top real estate agent will have a large rolodex that she will generously share with you. His vendor database will include top mortgage lenders, great escrow officers, and the very best home inspectors. Whether you need a moving company or a house cleaner, a great real estate agent is resourceful enough to have professionals they can recommend.

Reputation, Integrity, and Professionalism

You want an agent who reflects your values. What is more important than the integrity of a business professional with whom you share your intimate financial details? You will recognize the integrity of the people you work with because they will always put your interests first, ahead of their own. A real estate agent who is highly respected in her community will have a great reputation for service. When you meet a real estate agent, you can determine his level of professionalism by his appearance. You will soon know if this is someone you can count on.

What are the agents' colleagues saying about them? One great place to check is *ActiveRain,* which is a top blogging site for real estate agents and vendors across the United States. Another place to check references is on LinkedIn. What are their clients saying about them? It really does make a difference.

Member of local REALTOR® Association and MLS?

Verify that the REALTOR® you have chosen to interview is really a REALTOR®. In other words, is she a member of her National Association of REALTORS®, (NAR) her state association of REALTORS®, and her local association of REALTORS®? Some real estate agents are not REALTOR® members and therefore are not obligated to uphold high standards such as the REALTOR® code of ethics.

Has he joined his local MLS (Multiple Listing Service)? If not, he will not have access to the current houses for sale in your area. If a real estate agent is not a member of his local MLS (confidential agent database of houses for sale), how will you receive instant email alerts of new homes on the market? Make sure that your real estate agent has all the latest tools including access to the local MLS.

"Can Do" Attitude

How important is attitude? Extremely important! You need to choose a REALTOR® who can persevere despite obstacles; someone with a positive attitude. If your REALTOR® has good negotiating skills, you can feel confident that you will get a great deal with no hassles because she will go to bat for you. If there is a challenge, he will craft a solution. You need a professional with this type of fortitude and persistence to work on your behalf.

A person with a positive "can do" attitude will help your buying experience to be smooth and enjoyable. It is great to have a professional whom you know you can rely on, a person who always finds a way to solve any challenges. When you put your faith in a person like this as your team member, you know that things will always turn out for the best.

Research 5, Interview 3, Select 1

As always, our formula for hiring a great team member is to research 5, interview 3, and hire 1 person to work for you. You may have received great recommendations from friends and family members, and you may feel comfortable with the first agent that you interview. If so, hire her on the spot; and that's fine, too.

As we discussed, a real estate agent may have been faithfully sending you email alerts for the past several months. If so, I would encourage you to interview him first and give him the first opportunity to work for you, since he has already proven that he can do a great job for you.

During your transaction, if you have a problem with your agent, you should talk to the agent's broker. If it's still not resolved, you can contact their local Realtor® association. That's an important reason to make sure that your agent is a Realtor®. However, if you've received a good referral, done your research, and interviewed as we suggested, you shouldn't ever need to worry about firing your agent.

Agent and Client Loyalty

Once you have hired a buyer's agent to represent you, you expect that professional to work hard for you and act in your best interests. In return, you will be loyal to your buyer's agent. That means you will cooperate with the paperwork and communication. Also it means that you will not contact any other agents who may want to represent you. When you see Open Houses, online home searches, For Sale signs, and new home developments, make a note and then contact YOUR AGENT instead of the listing agent or the developer.

What better way to spend a Sunday afternoon than viewing model homes to get decorating tips... However, if you go to a new home development, you will be required to register as a guest. And that's where it gets sticky. If you later decide to purchase a home from that developer, they may not pay your Realtor®'s commission, which means your agent may not be able to represent you. In other words, you should make sure that you view new homes **WITH** your selected agent.

Now that we introduced you to the concepts needed for buying your first home, let's move on to Step 1 and continue the process.

STEP 1:
Prepare For Home Ownership

Now that we know home buying is a **process,** let's get ready with the first step: preparing ourselves. Write down your financial goals for yourselves and your family.

1. Write down financial goals
2. Prepare a monthly budget
3. Upgrade your credit score
4. Eliminate consumer debt
5. Save money
6. Take a course
7. Change your mind set

In order to accomplish your goals, you need to prepare a monthly budget for the entire year. Your main focus is that YOU want to be in control of your budget. Don't let your debt and bills control you!

It's critical to have a good credit score because without it, your mortgage lender would not approve your loan. Check your credit score and upgrade it so you can qualify for a more favorable loan, with the lowest interest rate and the best terms available.

You might be surprised to learn that half of your mortgage payment may be going towards interest payments instead of paying down the principal loan balance. That's why it's so important to start with the lowest interest rate possible, and pay down the principal as much as you can, as soon as possible.

Of course, we want to eliminate as much debt as possible, and we will discuss how to pay off your credit cards and loans. Debt consolidation is a great start to paying off your bill and becoming debt-free. By getting rid of debt, you will feel relieved because you won't have as many bills to pay. You will also be able to qualify for a larger loan, and, therefore, you can buy a better home.

We will discuss how to save money for your home. Even if you're going to get a zero-down loan with 100% financing, you will need some funds saved up. You may need to pay closing costs, home inspection, or upgrades to the home. Learn to be a good steward over your financial resources and you will feel better about yourself because you will be in control of your future!

It is important to get educated about home ownership. Congratulations, you are on the right path because you are already reading this book! Be sure to make good notes so you can refer back to these steps later on.

Change your mindset and your vision. Picture yourself as a homeowner, not a renter. Start by visualizing yourself in your own home. What type of neighborhood will you live in? What will your home look like? How excited will you feel when you design it in your favorite style? How grateful will you be each month when you pay your mortgage loan? Think how peaceful your family will be when they can relax and enjoy their own home.

When is the best time to buy a home? It is now! However, it doesn't happen overnight, so start preparing today. Simply start with Step 1 and as long as you follow the path, you WILL become a homeowner. It may be 2 months from now, 6 months later, or a year down the road. I have helped many renters become first-time homebuyers, and I know that if you follow our step-by-step plan, your dream of home ownership WILL come true!

1. Write Down Financial Goals

Let's discuss your financial goals that typically include:

- Saving money
- Owning a home
- Paying off debts
- Earning more income
- Contributing to worthy charities

Write out Both Short-Term and Long-Term Goals

Obviously, becoming a homeowner is at the top of your list. That's why you're reading our book!

When do you want to be debt-free - 1 year, 5 years, 10 years, 20 years, or 30 years from now?

When are you going to pay off your student loans? When will you buy a house? How much money will you save for your children's college fund? What year will you retire? How much monthly income will you need when you retire?

These are important questions to think about in order to start the planning process.

I suggest you create a "dream board", which is a poster or large paper with pictures of your vision. Find magazine photos of houses you like and glue them to your dream board. What about a photo of your children and your college hopes for them, travel and vacations? Definitely show what retirement will look like for you.

<u>For example</u>:

- Buy a house within 1 year
- Be debt-free within 5 years
- Save up for children's college in 10 years
- Pay off mortgage in 20 years
- Retire in 30 years

Of course, you cannot do everything at once, so you need to prioritize. Think about it and figure out which goals are most important. Which should you work toward first? I believe that owning a home is a cornerstone of that plan. Home ownership will give you financial stability and you will then be able to start working toward your other goals. Remember that after your mortgage is paid, you will not have a monthly house payment and then you can retire completely debt-free!

Get the *Entire Family* Involved in this Process!

If everyone is focused on the same goals, then it is easier to make sacrifices together. I recommend having a family meeting every week to allow communication, commitment, and accountability. If you are a family of 1 (in other words, you are single), get a friend who will consult with you each week regarding your financial goals. Have a regular time for your weekly meeting.

To start, why not call a family meeting right away and get everyone's input and commitment to your goals? Where can each person make sacrifices? For example, can we cut out some of the entertainment expenses by having a family movie night — renting a movie and making popcorn at home instead of paying $50 to go to the movie theater?

Look at your dining out, coffee, and snack expenses. You will be shocked at how quickly the Starbucks and fast food bills add up. To save money, simply prepare your coffee and meals at home, ahead of time. That requires some advance planning.

2. Prepare Your Monthly Budget

It is time to pencil in your monthly budget. Your budget will help show you how much income you have coming in, what expenses are going out, how much you are putting aside for savings, and how much extra money you have left after your bills are paid. The extra money is called *"disposable income"*.

If your income is too low, can you find ways to earn more income? If your expenses are too high, how can you cut out some of them? If you have credit cards and other consumer debt, how can you pay them off? How will you put aside money and save up funds to buy your home?

A budget form that you can use to track and manage your finances is located in the back of this guide. It is organized into categories so you can quickly see how much money is going toward housing, transportation, food, health care, children, and other things. You can more easily determine if you are wasting money that could be saved instead.

If you do not know what your monthly expenses are, then you need to start tracking your expenses. Get a handle on your expenses by keeping receipts for EVERYTHING you spend and put them into a box or folder. At the end of the month, tally up your expenses. It only takes an hour or two each month to calculate your budget.

Your Housing Payment Should be Maximum 1/3 of your Monthly Income

For a renter, that would be your rent payment plus your utilities. When you become a homeowner, it will include your mortgage, taxes, and insurance, plus HOA fees if you have them in your community. Remember to put aside money for ongoing maintenance and repairs.

Your Monthly Debts Should Be No More Than 10% to 15% of your Gross Monthly Income

Debts include student loans, car payments, child support, and consumer debt such as credit cards. Anything that shows up on your credit report, including old bills that went to collection, will be included in the calculation of your income to debt ratio. That is the ideal, but most of us have quite a bit more debt than we would like. So I would challenge you to pay off as many debts as possible and put yourself into a better financial position.

Eliminate Debts and Expenses if You Can

Once you start keeping track of entertainment, recreation, and extracurricular activities, you will be surprised how much of your budget is eaten up in these categories. Other hidden money pit drains include late fees, bank overdraft charges, payday loans, cell phone overages, traffic tickets, and miscellaneous cash purchases from out of pocket.

What else can you cut out of your budget? Recreation, vacation, and travel can be cut way back. It does not mean you won't have any fun in your life, it simply means that you can discover new cost-effective ways to enjoy life and have adventures for a while. It is a small sacrifice but really, really worth it.

This is known as the principle of *"delayed gratification"*. If you are willing to sacrifice a little bit right now, just think of all the recreational trips and vacations you will have later when you are retired and completely debt-free. So get everyone's buy-in and by working together, you can reach your goals.

Income Fluctuation

Advice for 2-income families: a good rule of thumb is to buy what you can afford with only 1 income. Of course, you probably won't get the most luxurious home, but you'll have stability knowing that you will be able to survive any future life decision or financial hurdle.

I often see young buyers (with no children) purchase a large, expensive home that requires 2 incomes. After they move in, the wife gets pregnant and decides to stop working so she can be a full-time mom at home with her baby. Unfortunately, she can't stop working because the mortgage payment is excessive. So she is forced to decide: either be away from her baby all day, or downsize to a less expensive house.

Moms often decide to quit working once they have babies. So ask yourself: can you handle your mortgage payment on only 1 income? Think about the future. We advise you to think long-term and not limit yourself. Don't commit to such a large monthly payment that you are trapped into both mom and dad working full-time forever. Give yourself some room for future flexibility.

When we were young, our mom was so great with saving money and she taught us valuable lessons about living within our means. Her favorite saying was, "Use what you have." In other words, instead of running to the store to buy something, look around at what you already have and think about a creative way you can adapt to solve your situation.

She was also thinking of creative solutions to stretch our budget further. One year, she purchased a truck with a camper for our family vacations. She bought it with money she had saved, rather than purchasing the truck on credit.

We took a lot of fun trips throughout the years, and were able to view many historic sites in California. We have great memories of visiting California caverns at Angels Camp, the Yosemite waterfalls, the gold rush town of Columbia, Hearst Castle, and the giant Redwood trees at Big Sur. Since we traveled in our camper, we did not have to pay for a hotel room or for restaurants. Now that is vacationing on a budget!

You Should Be Saving Money Every Month

Put aside money for your "rainy day" emergency fund. I suggest that at least 10% of your income go directly to savings. It is a relief to know that if your car breaks down or if you get sick, you have some savings to draw from, and you don't have to take money from important bills like your housing or transportation. If you are not currently saving money, hold a family meeting and get everyone to make sacrifices to work towards your goal.

Contact your Financial Advisor or Planner for Assistance

Remember that your budget is not set in stone; it will change over time, so allow for flexibility. The main idea is to monitor your finances, and make adjustments to stay on track to meet your goal.

I recommend that you contact your financial advisor or planner for assistance. If you do not yet have one, take the time to research 5, interview 3, and select 1 who can help you. A financial planner is a licensed professional who can assist you in reaching your family's goals.

3. Upgrade Your Credit Score

Don't be fooled by ads on TV that make you think they will give you a free credit report. There is always a catch! The government requires the credit reporting bureaus to provide 1 free report each year, and they provide a web site where you can get a free report without any strings attached. It is not the web site you see on TV.

Get Copies of your 3 Credit Reports Free at www.AnnualCreditReport.com

You are going to want to upgrade your credit score before you purchase a house and the best place to start is to get a free copy of your credit report at *www.AnnualCreditReport.com*. Remember there are 3 different credit bureaus, so each credit agency is going to have different information. This is the web site for the consumer's copy of the free reports as mandated by the government, but it does not include your FICO scores.

Check your FICO Score at www.MyFico.com

The FICO score is a number between 300 and 850 that lenders use to determine your credit risk. Scores are calculated based on payment history, debts owed, and the types of credit used. However, you can get a free FICO score from 1 of the credit bureaus with your trial membership at www.MyFico.com. That should give you a good idea of how you rank for loan scoring purposes.

FICO Scores

- 750 - 800 = A Excellent
- 700 – 750 = B Above Average
- 620 – 700 = C Average
- 580 – 620 = D Below Average
- Below 580 = F Poor

It is similar to your school grade teacher grading your tests as A, B, C, D, or F. The better your FICO score, the better loan rate and terms you qualify for. Most loans will require a 650 score or above, which is average, like a "C". Scores of 700 and above are above average, like a "B", and scores over 750 are excellent, which is similar to an "A". Scores under 620 are considered below average, like a "D". This type of credit score puts you in subprime territory, and you will have a difficult time finding a mortgage loan. Anything under 580 is an "F", which means you definitely would not be able to qualify for a loan right now.

A FICO score is comprised of these elements, which are weighted according to the list below:

- Your payment history (35% of the score)
- How much debt you owe (30% of the score)
- How many years your credit has been established (15% of the score)
- The types of credit you use (10% of the score)
- Whether you have any new credit accounts (10% of the score)

To find out about credit reports and how to improve your FICO score, visit the Fair Isaac website for consumers at **www.MyFico.com**.

Review the Reports for Accuracy

It is important to review your credit reports for accuracy. Many people do not realize that credit reports often contain errors. The Consumer Federation of America and the National Credit Reporting Association say that more than a third of consumers could be hurt by the errors or omissions in credit reports (The Augusta Chronicle, 2002). So go through each item, especially those that are negatively impacting your report, and determine if there are any mistakes.

> *"No matter how good the mathematics of credit scoring, it's based on information in your credit report – which may be, and frequently is, wrong. Sometimes the errors are small or irrelevant... Other times the problems are significant... Many people discover this misinformation only after they've been turned down for credit." p.9 (Weston, 2012)*

Correct Erroneous and Unresolved Items

A few derogatory items can make your credit report dip way down from a "B" to a "D". Clear up unresolved items right away, such as defaulted student loans or charge-offs.

Once you receive your free credit report from **www.AnnualCreditReport.com**, you can respond back and they will automatically review your disputed items. However, I have noticed that since it is a computerized review, you really don't have the opportunity to explain your story, or to show proof of errors. It does not appear that a real person actually reviews these disputes, as my experience has shown that their computer may send you a response saying that they "confirmed it was all correct" and they won't change your report.

If you do not get a satisfactory response online, consider pursuing other options. You can mail a formal written letter to the credit bureau, following the consumer laws, and follow up continually to monitor their progress. When you mail in a letter, they are more likely to have a real person review your report instead of a computer robot.

> *"The credit bureaus handle billions of pieces of data every day, so to some extent errors, outdated information, and missing information are inevitable – but the credit-reporting system often makes it difficult to get rid of errors after you spot them." p.9 (Weston, 2012)*

Another option is to hire a professional credit counselor to go to bat for you and negotiate with the credit bureau's legal department. It may cost you a bit of money, but if you can remove erroneous items and get approved for your mortgage loan, it is worth it!

Improve your Credit Score

Pay all credit payments on time for at least 6 months. Pay down revolving debt to 30% of your credit limit. The best way to improve your score is to pay all credit payments on time for at least 6 months and to pay down revolving debt to maximum 30% of the credit limit. If your credit limit is $1,000, for example, you keep your balance under $300. Each month, pay MORE than the minimum payment to your credit accounts. As you pay on time, and pay down your balances, you will see your score begin to build up.

Other great tips are: DO NOT apply for any new accounts and DO NOT open new credit accounts. When you have your credit report run by a merchant, or when you open a new account, your score may drop down. It is tempting to buy things on credit, but don't. If you cannot afford the item with the money you have already saved up, you probably do not need to buy it.

Think about your goal of home ownership and how important your dream is to you and your family. Be willing to live on less and to sacrifice little things so you can have the big things that really matter!

4. Eliminate Consumer Debt

Get your credit card balances as low as possible, and your consumer debt paid off. What are the best ways to eliminate consumer debt?

- Pay off consumer debt by making extra principal payments
- Do NOT make any purchases on credit
- Do NOT apply for credit cards

Pay off Consumer Debt by Making Additional Principal Payments

The next step is to eliminate consumer debt by paying off as much as possible. If you cannot pay it off right away, make substantial payments to reduce your debts. Some people would advise you not to pay off your credit cards and close the accounts, because you need to have some type of monthly payments that demonstrate your capacity to pay on time, thus building your credit score. If you have several credit cards, get rid of them as you pay them off. Keep only 1 or 2 cards for rainy day emergencies.

By the way, which credit card account should you keep open? Probably the one you have had for the longest period, since it shows the longest credit history. Keep that 1 credit card that you have had a long time and have always paid on time. Pay it way, way down (below 30% of your credit limit) or pay it off each month if you can.

The Scriptures say: *"Just as the rich rule the poor, so the borrower is servant to the lender."* The lesson is that debt is an entrapment because, until your debt is paid off, you are obligated to that lender.

Here is my challenge to you: Pay off your consumer debt this year. Consumer debt is any credit account you use to buy electronic goods, household furniture, clothing and jewelry, Christmas presents, take vacations, or purchase anything that is not an asset.

Your house is an asset that should be appreciating in value. On the other hand, consumer goods are personal items that only DECREASE in value.

What about your car? Does it ever increase in value? Unfortunately not; its value diminishes every day also. If you went into debt to purchase large "toys" such as RVs, boats, jet skis, or quads, sell them now and pay off the associated debt. Remember, the more debt you have, the less house you can afford to buy!

Do NOT Purchase an Automobile or Make Any Other Major Purchases on Credit

When you apply for credit before your loan is funded, you risk your loan being denied and therefore jeopardize your home purchase. Remember, the lender is going to pull your credit again shortly before closing, and examine it to verify if it is still the same as when you initially applied for your loan.

I once had a friend who was so excited to buy her first home. I was helping her with the purchase and giving her guidance on the home-buying process. The day before escrow was scheduled to close, I received a call from the escrow officer. "Nina's loan has been withdrawn by the lender so we're not closing tomorrow." What? That was just plain crazy.

I called the lender to yell at him. What was up? I wanted to know. He said, "We just ran her credit again, and guess what showed up on her report... a new charge account at a local furniture store for $10,000. She was already borderline, but now her debt ratio is too high. I am sorry but she does not qualify for the loan any more. The underwriter has revoked the loan approval." She did NOT do that!

I know that Nina would never jeopardize her dream home. I could not believe what my ears were hearing so I quickly called her to find out if it was true.

"Yes," she admitted. "I got so excited about our new home and besides, we needed new furniture. I didn't want to have old furniture in our brand new home."

As I explained the consequences of her actions, her heart sank. Well, the good news is that I was able to talk to the lender and get them to approve her loan again.

However, they did have to increase her interest rate because the higher debt amount put her into a higher risk category.

Although this story has a good ending, yours may not. So please, while you are in the process of buying your home, do not do ANYTHING to disturb your credit or your financial situation. Do not buy anything on credit, especially not furniture or appliances. Do not spend the down payment that you have saved. Do not quit your job or change jobs (unless it is a promotion at the same company) because you need a 2-year work history. Do not even change bank accounts!

Your Lender Calculates your Debt Ratios

Your debt ratio determines how much "house" you can afford. If you are going to change your credit score or your debt ratios, change them for the better. You want to owe as little money as possible. The reason is that all of your monthly debts are counted against you. Your lender calculates your debt ratios to determine how much "house" you can afford.

There is a "front end" ratio which is your total housing payment, and then a "back end" ratio which is your housing payment PLUS all your monthly consumer debts. These debts are measured against your monthly income and are calculated as a ratio.

For a conventional loan, the front-end ratio is 28% and the back end ratio is 36%. However, with compensating factors the ratios can be approved at higher rates. For FHA loans, the ratios are generally 38% and 43%, and again, with compensating factors the rates can be slightly higher.

For example, if your family household income is $5,000 per month and you are applying for an FHA loan, then a front-end ratio of 38% would be $1,900 maximum monthly housing payment. That includes your mortgage payment, taxes, insurance, and any other housing fees such as HOA or PMI. A back end ratio of 43% would mean your total housing payments plus other debts could only be maximum $2,150 per month.

If you subtract a $1,900 housing payment from the maximum debt of $2,150, you only have $250 per month available to pay your car loans, student loans, and all other monthly debts combined. That is not much leeway! This is a great reason why we are teaching you to keep your debt as low as possible.

The ratios applied by your lender will depend on the type of loan you are receiving, and what banking program or government agency will be guaranteeing the loan. Some ratios are more generous, while others are stricter. Your mortgage lender will be knowledgeable about the different programs and will help you select the best loan program for your situation.

5. Save Money

Start saving now! You will need to save money for the following types of home buying expenses:

- Credit report fee
- Earnest money deposit (EMD)
- Total down payment
- Home inspections
- Appraisal
- Closing costs

You will Need Money to Purchase your Home

The next logical step is to save money. As you remember, you put your budget together, and you saw items that you could stop spending money on, and eliminate from budget. Then you could take that money and put it back into your savings account.

I know what you are thinking right now. You are saying, "I have a zero down payment loan with 100% financing. Why do I need to save money?" Well, even if your loan is financed 100% by the bank, you may have closing costs, inspections, and reports.

More importantly, you will need to put down an earnest money deposit to open escrow, which is typically $1,000 or sometimes even more. This gives the sellers "good faith" that you will perform as agreed. I would suggest saving up at least $2,000 for a zero-down loan, and you will need to save even more if you have a loan with 3.5% down, 10% down, or 20% down.

Want to know another good reason to start saving your money? With some loans, the lender will want to have assurance that you can pay your mortgage every month. They may require that you have 2 months of cash reserves on hand. That means you must have at least 2 months' worth of your total housing payment in your savings account at the bank. No, you cannot simply borrow money from your parents and put it into your bank account. The lender will need you to show that the funds are "seasoned". In other words, the funds must have been in your bank account for at least several months.

You will Need to Make Sacrifices by Cutting Back

This is where you may need to cut back your spending and make some sacrifices. What expenses can you eliminate?

One of the biggest areas of concern that I see is families eating out way too often. Add up the cost that you spend on dining out, whether it is fast food, restaurant take-out, or dining in. You will probably be shocked at how much you waste eating outside the home.

I know it seems easier to eat out because we are all busy with our on-the-go lifestyles and there is a fast food restaurant on every corner.

TIP: Prepare your meal in a crock-pot in the morning, and it will be easier to pass up the fast food when you know that a delicious homemade meal is waiting for you at home later that night.

I am a busy working mom too, and I know it is challenging to come home tired from working all day, and then cook dinner for your family. When you are driving by a fast food place, it seems easier to pick up dinner on the go...especially when you are hungry and you smell the food cooking. However, you can save a lot of money by preparing fresh food at home every day.

That means shopping once a week for fresh produce, perhaps even visiting your local farmer's market for seasonal fruits and veggies. It means planning ahead and writing out a menu in advance.

It means preparing your lunches ahead of time at home, such as making sandwiches, soup, or salad. As a side benefit, you and your family will have better nutrition, too. You will be sick less and feel much healthier.

Another huge drain on the budget is that "little" coffee habit. If you spend $5 per day at Starbucks, did you know that is $1,825 per year? Over 10 years, that adds up to $18,250. Over the life of your 40 working years, spending merely $5 per day adds up to $73,000. So look at what you are spending on coffee, snacks, alcohol, and fast food. It can add up to a staggering amount of money, which should be going back into your household bank account.

We already discussed those "hidden" money drains, such as credit card late fees, returned check overdraft charges (*NSF*, "not sufficient funds") from your bank, and cell phone charges for over-minutes-usage. If you add it up, you may be shocked how much you waste on needless fees every year. It is like taking your hard-earned paycheck and flushing it down the drain.

Lastly, I do not have to remind you that if you still have any secret "vices" or addictions, stop them immediately! Break your costly habits such as gambling, cigarettes, porn, alcohol, drugs, and tattoos and put that money right into your budget. You will save money instantly. You will feel better about yourself, and your family will thank you, too.

Save for the Biggest Downpayment Possible

For your downpayment, put down as much cash as you possibly can. The larger your downpayment, the lower your monthly payments.

A large downpayment gives you many benefits:

- You may qualify for a better mortgage loan
- It puts your offer in a more competitive light for the seller to accept your offer
- Your monthly mortgage payment will be lower
- It may eliminate the need for PMI
- You earn more equity starting from the close of escrow
- It improves your credit score due to lower LTV ratio
- You are committed to your home because your vested interest is larger

Your next question probably is — where do you get the money for your down payment? Let's discuss several sources of funds. First of all, you do NOT want to borrow money for your down payment. Whether it's a loan from family or it's against your retirement account, it would be poor money management to have additional debt ON TOP of your mortgage loan. That's the quickest way to get deep in debt shortly after close of escrow. So think about creative ways you can come up with cash.

1. **Savings account**. Start saving a portion of your paycheck automatically every month with payroll deduction. Your local credit union can help you set this up.
2. **Gift from your parents** — a certain amount may be tax deductible. Again, this is NOT a loan, it would be a gift. (However, there may be strings attached: your parents may want to help you select the house.)
3. **Bonus or commission from your job**. Either a year-end bonus or a one-time bonus will really help. Sock it away and resist the temptation to spend it!
4. **Tax refund** — again, put this right into your savings without spending it.
5. **Sell your "toys"**. Start with big-ticket toys, such as trailer, boat, RV, quads, jet skis. This will also help you reduce your consumer debt. If you're having trouble prying these toys loose, ask yourself what's a bigger priority: toys or your own home?
6. **Have a yard sale** and get rid of everything you haven't used recently. You'll be surprised how much "stuff" you've accumulated - and how relieved you'll feel when it's cleaned out. As a side benefit, this will give you a fresh start in your new home — and less stuff you have to move!
7. **Downpayment assistance programs** — available through local cities, counties, government programs, non-profit organizations, and also some banks.
8. Consider **working overtime** for 3 months to generate some extra one-time cash. I do not advise it long term because you'll get burned out. But if overtime work is available on a short-term basis, grab it and log in those extra hours. Then be diligent about putting that extra money aside for your downpayment.
9. **Cash out your accrued vacation pay**, sick pay, or bonuses. Often employees will lose their accumulated vacation if they don't use it, so maybe you can convert it to

cash. However, I would not advise you to deplete your retirement funds...that's not a good long-term strategy.

While you're considering creative ways to come up with cash, there are some things you DON'T want to do. Do not rob your retirement or your children's college savings account. You will need these funds for the future.

How do You Keep Focused on your Priority?

When you focus on your goal of home ownership, it is easy to see what priorities are most important. Does budgeting and saving take a little more work? Yes, but the rewards are worth the sacrifices!

Being a responsible homeowner is about discipline, and you will feel at peace when you have the self-discipline to make little sacrifices to meet your big goals. Ask yourself and your family: Do we want to be renters 5 years from now? 10 years from now? 20 or even 30 years from now?

If home ownership is an important goal, what are you each willing to do to make it work? Put up a photo of your dream home and visualize your new home together as a family. Instead of discussing "if" you will get your home, talk about what you will do "when" you buy your home. See your home and your goal. You can make it real!

6. Enroll in Home Buying Course

The most important thing you will learn is that home buying is a **PROCESS**. You'll become familiar with the steps, the terms, the forms. The more courses you participate in, the more confidence you will gain to take action.

Learn about Home Ownership and the Process of Buying a House

Take an educational course to learn about how to buy a home, and what it takes to own a home. It is quite a process and when you own a home, you will have different responsibilities than when you were a renter. There are steps to follow and it is not instant.

Take a First-Time Homebuyer Course Offered in your Community

Attend a homebuyer course offered in your community. The U.S. Department of Housing and Urban Development (HUD) offers an eight-hour workshop that you can take through certified non-profit housing organizations in major metro areas.

To find a Home Buyer counseling agency in your area, go to *www.HUD.gov and search for "HUD Approved Housing Counseling Agencies"*.

If you are receiving a grant or down payment assistance, you may be required to complete a HUD course in order to qualify for it. If so, take the course with a positive attitude. Be open and willing to learn. At the workshop, take plenty of notes and find out as much as you can.

Educate Yourself

In addition, many of these nonprofit organizations offer free or low-cost one-on-one counseling sessions where you and your spouse can talk to a certified, trained counselor in private.

Search for homeownership topics on the internet. Whether you have a question about the appraisal, the home inspection, or the title insurance, you are sure to find lots of information posted in various blogs, and perhaps you will even find suggestions from recent homebuyers.

You are Learning Right Now!

Most importantly, you have already taken the first step to home ownership by reading this guide book today. Congratulations to you! Give yourself a big hand for taking the next step forward and realizing your dream.

7. Change Your Mindset

In what way is a homeowner more responsible than a renter?

- Homeowners pay mortgage, taxes, and insurance
- Homeowners must maintain their own yard
- Homeowners will have to repair plumbing if it leaks

Remember, a homeowner also gets more rewards and long-term financial benefits. Homeowners are focused on security, stability, and holding onto assets for their future generations.

Being a Homeowner Requires a Different Mindset than Renting

Just as we discussed earlier, being a homeowner requires a different mindset than being a renter. If you are a renter, you sit back and wait for the landlord to fix things. You do not have to worry about the mortgage being paid or the cost of repairs.

However, when you are a homeowner, you take active charge of your house. When something breaks, you cannot just call your landlord. You take active responsibility, you take care of things and you get them fixed.

Therefore, being a renter and being a homeowner are 2 different mindsets. One is expecting someone else to do things, and the other is doing it yourself for your family. Being a homeowner means you are investing your time, energy, and money into your own house.

You are Responsible for the Maintenance and Repairs

Home ownership may mean learning how to do repairs yourself. It may mean finding reliable contractors. It may mean calling your brother-in-law, the handyman, to come help you in exchange for a barbecue dinner. Buildings and yards require maintenance, so you are going to have a little bit different attitude. When something needs to be repaired, you cannot just call your landlord any more.

Maintenance should be done on a regular basis. Things that need to be replaced should be put into your schedule: such as, clean the rain gutters; replace leaky water faucets and toilets; check, repair, and replace the roof; replace the hot water heater, replace worn-out light fixtures; put in new appliances; clean vents and heating ducts; and check water pressure.

Most repairs can be avoided simply by doing preventive maintenance. Otherwise, repairs will be needed, and your small leak could suddenly turn into a flooded bathroom.

You must Plan Ahead for your Expenses

Your mortgage is the most important bill you pay each month. It keeps a roof over your head. Therefore, plan ahead for your mortgage, taxes, and insurance expenses. Pay them before you pay any other bills. If your lender is impounding your taxes and insurance into an escrow account, then you do not need to pay them separately.

Most homeowners have to pay taxes and insurance twice a year, which means planning and putting those expenses into your budget. Remember to put money aside for maintenance, repairs and improvements. Plan in advance and schedule them into your budget.

Start to Think Long Term

Homeowners are more focused on their family's stability in the long term. They dream of retiring one day and have a plan to get there.

Remember when you were shopping for houses and you found that one house that was stuck in the 1970's? The homes with the avocado green shag carpet, the pink bathtub, and the mustard yellow tiles on the kitchen counters?

You were wondering, "Why didn't these homeowners upgrade their house in the last 40 years?" Maybe it is because they did not budget for upgrades up front. Don't get stuck decades behind; instead, plan ahead for your improvements. It will keep the value of your home high. It will put some excitement in your life and keep you from getting bored of your house.

More importantly, it will keep you from feeling as if you have to move to another house just because yours is outdated and you have grown weary of it.

Being able to improve and upgrade your home is one of the huge benefits of owning your own home.

STEP 2:
Get Ready to Shop for Houses

Are you ready to buy a house? It's time to get excited! Let's get ready to shop for houses. House shopping is the most exciting, and interesting, part of buying a house.

1. Research neighborhoods
2. Interview lender
3. Give documents to the lender
4. Get pre-qualified
5. Calculate your monthly payment
6. Work toward receiving a pre-approval letter
7. Sign the buyer rep agreement
8. Include decision-makers
9. Search new listings on the market
10. Drive by the houses you select

First, we are going to research neighborhoods to find out where we want to live, where the best schools are, and where our family wants to live.

Second, we are going to interview lenders to find out about what type of mortgage loans are available for us. What is the interest rate? What is our monthly payment, and what does it include?

Third, we are going to copy documents and give them to the lender. We will show you what you need to be prepared for that important lender appointment.

Fourth, we are going to get pre-qualified with the best mortgage lender based on our income and credit.

Fifth, we are going to calculate the monthly payment, which will include all of our housing costs. That will help us determine exactly how much we can afford in our budget, and what price of house we will buy.

Sixth, we are going to get that pre-qualification letter in our hand, ready to make an offer. Once we have the pre-qualification letter, we will work toward receiving a pre-approval letter.

Seventh, we are going to sign the Buyer/Broker Representation agreement with our REALTOR® so he can represent us as his client and take our family house shopping.

Eighth, we will need to include any decision-makers in our family because we want to agree. We want to select the best house for everyone who has a vested interest in our home purchase.

Ninth, we are going to keep track of new listings as they come on the market for sale. Our REALTOR® will put us on an email alert system for houses that meet our search criteria.

Finally, we are going to select our favorite new listings and drive by the neighborhood to eliminate those we do NOT want to view. This is going to be a huge time-saver when we are shopping with our REALTOR® and making our first offer.

Are you ready? Let's go!

1. Research Neighborhoods

Why should you and your family research neighborhoods by driving around communities you want to live in?

- Find out about the schools and services that are important to you
- Eliminate areas where you do not want to live
- Compare communities and their amenities

Drive Around Neighborhoods Where you Would Like to Live

Remember I said you were going to have to do a little footwork yourself? This assignment is your family's homework.

The first thing you are going to do is to research the various neighborhoods in your price range. Now, if you already live in a single-family house in a community that you like, and your children are already enrolled in school here, then this is probably a neighborhood where you want to live.

However, perhaps you cannot afford this neighborhood because the home prices are out of your range. If so, be open to relocating to a new neighborhood that fits within your homebuyer budget. This is where your research comes in handy.

Find out About Schools, Services, and Other Statistics

Besides driving around, ask co-workers or church friends to recommend areas they like. Where do your friends live? What do they like best about their community? What are the downfalls of particular neighborhoods? Start by researching these neighborhoods on the internet.

It's always wise to select a home in a good school district. Property in a great school district is more valuable, so research the school ratings carefully. You can find information about schools at **www.GreatSchools.com**.

> *"If you have children, or plan to, then the quality of the local school district is probably high on your list. But even if you don't plan on children, you should be concerned with school quality, because the next family who buys your home might want children. And they'll pay more if the local schools are great."* p.75 (Bray, 2011)

You can ask your real estate agent for neighborhood suggestions, but she may not be able to give you all the answers you are seeking. The reason is that real estate agents must obey certain laws, so they cannot "steer" you toward a neighborhood or away from a neighborhood.

For example, agents won't report the racial composition of a neighborhood. They cannot give you their opinion of a "bad" or a "good" neighborhood, and they can't recommend certain areas where cultural or religious groups of people live (or do not live). They cannot tell you which school districts are better and which are worse. Agents are careful to comply with fair housing laws.

One last tip: As you are driving around neighborhoods, you will see "For Sale" signs on houses. Write down the address, but do NOT call the agent on the sign. If you try to call the listing agent whose name is on the sign, he won't be able to help you since you are already working with a real estate agent.

Instead, call the REALTOR® you have already hired and allow her to look up the price and details in the MLS (Multiple Listing Service) for you.

Eliminate Areas Where You Do NOT Want to Live

It is up to YOU to research the neighborhoods. School districts post their ratings online and police departments post their crime statistics online, so it's simple to research that data. You can also discover demographic data by zip codes, such as: average household income, educational level, and family size.

To feel the atmosphere of a neighborhood, I suggest you drive around during various times of the day, the evening, workdays, and weekends. If you don't feel safe driving around a neighborhood, that's a huge red flag that you certainly are not going to move your family there.

How close do you want to be to the downtown area? What types of recreation, parks, and entertainment are nearby? What about shopping and restaurants? Is it close to your job? What is the school district like? Will the children have to change schools? Is it near a freeway? How far away from Grandma and Grandpa?

Your goal is find a few neighborhoods that you like, and to eliminate certain areas from your home search. Tell your REALTOR® what you have found and get some feedback on various areas. Remember, the decision is up to you, because ultimately you and your family will be living there.

Compare Communities and Their Amenities

Things to look for include: signs of a well-established community; a neighborhood that is being maintained by the city; and residents who care.

To meet my criteria, I would want the streets to be paved with no potholes. I would want to see a curb and gutter system and sidewalks well maintained. I would want to see streetlights that come on at night, mature trees that provide shade during the summer, and front lawns watered and mowed.

I would hope that most residents would have jobs and be at work during the day, but in the evening, the air would be filled with the aroma of homemade dinner cooking in the oven.

In the late afternoons, I would expect to see kids riding their bikes or playing ball together. On the weekends, I would want to see residents mowing their lawns, walking their dogs, or pushing baby strollers.

I would look for amenities nearby such as a local restaurant, an elementary school within walking distance, a corner deli or mini-mart, a community park for the kids, and a church within a mile or so.

Try waving to the neighbors just to see how friendly they are. These are all signs of a good neighborhood and I would consider moving my family here. I have even been known to visit a new school and sit in on a few classes before I decide if I want to move my children to this school.

2. Interview Lenders

Almost all first home buyers will acquire a mortgage loan to help them purchase their new property. A few buyers will purchase with all cash, and no mortgage financing. But in high-cost areas like the California coast, it's usually necessary to get a mortgage loan. So you'll need to find a great mortgage lender for your team.

A few buyers are blessed with the ability to pay ALL CASH, and if that's your situation, terrific!!! If you are one of the few lucky families who can buy with all cash and you don't need a mortgage loan, kudos to you! You will have financial security and peace of mind. Living debt-free allows you to NOT worry about the economy and your job.

About Mortgage Loans and Lenders

Some buyers are able to get the seller to finance their home purchase, but most sellers are not in a position to finance the loan. Perhaps you're thinking about asking the seller to finance your home by taking back a loan for part of the purchase price. Seller financing is called "seller carry back" and it was previously a common type of "creative financing". Today this "creative financing" technique isn't utilized very often. If the seller does help you, make sure you get the loan prepared by a qualified attorney, and get the note properly recorded at close of escrow.

Most likely, you will need to get a mortgage loan. Sources of mortgage lending include big banks, small local banks, credit unions, mortgage brokerages, and non-profit organizations. So how do you interview and select a good mortgage lender to work with? We suggest that you hire your lender based on:

- The loan programs their company offers and the lender's knowledge of each program
- The lender's communication and working style
- Their track record and reputation for being prompt and efficient
- High recommendation from a friend who has used their services
- Extensive experience with first-time buyers

Select a mortgage lender who is a member of a respected professional association. Just like your real estate agent should belong to his or her local REALTOR® association, verify that your mortgage lender is a member of a professional association for mortgage lenders which upholds high standards. Below are professional associations:

- NAMP National Association of Mortgage Professionals - *www.namp.org*
- NAMB National Association of Mortgage Bankers - *www.namb.org*
- MBAA Mortgage Bankers Association - *www.mbaa.org*

These organizations emphasize that their members uphold high ethical and professional standards. Because they require accountability, the borrowers benefit from higher quality service standards. By hiring a lender who belongs to a professional industry organization, you can be confident that he or she upholds high quality standards.

Referral from your REALTOR®

Now you are going to interview mortgage lenders to find a great professional who can help you get qualified to purchase your new home. You are going to ask your real estate agent whom she would recommend. That is always the best place to start. Why? Your REALTOR® serves many first-time homebuyers and works closely with top lenders who are experienced in serving families like yours. She can refer to lenders who have low down payment programs, and help you get down payment assistance, or affordable closing costs.

Recommended by Friends, Family, or Co-workers

Also, ask your friends, family, and co-workers whom they recommend as a good mortgage lender. They may have had a recent experience with a lender they like. Ask around. Word of mouth is the best type of recommendation possible. I suggest that you find and research 5 lenders.

Set an Appointment and Interview 3 Lenders

Once you have found 5 lenders, narrow it down to 3 whom you want to interview. It will be easy to eliminate 2 from your list of 5 — they will be the ones who never call you back! I like to review business people on *www.Linkedin.com* to find out about their professional background. It is a great way to find out about their experience and to review recommendations about that person.

Make an appointment to go into the lender's office and meet for about 1 hour. Be sure it is a time when you and your spouse will both be available. If you are not married and someone else is signing on the loan with you, the co-signer should meet with the lender also.

Discover their Loan Programs and Working Style

When interviewing prospective lenders, ask each of them the same type of questions. See how they respond. Here are some things to ask them and evaluate, so take these questions with you to your interview.

- What type of loan programs do they offer? Federal Housing Administration (FHA), U.S. Department of Veterans Affairs (VA), U.S. Department of Agriculture (USDA)?
- Are they familiar with down payment assistance programs? Can they help you pay for closing costs?
- What are their rates compared to other lenders? Do they charge upfront fees? What are their initial loan fees? How much will they charge you for a credit report and an appraisal?
- Will your monthly payment be an all-inclusive payment, which includes taxes and insurance or will you have to pay those separately?
- How often is he available to answer your questions? Does his communication style work with yours? For example, does he prefer phone, email, or text message?
- How many years has she been licensed? Has her license always been maintained in good standing? Does she attend continuing education courses to further his knowledge?
- How many first-time homebuyers does he serve? What are some of his success stories? Does he have recommendations from any of his clients?
- Will she sit down and explain all the paperwork with you? Will she be there to answer your questions when you sign the loan documents?
- Is he responsive in returning your calls right away? Does he have an upbeat, cheerful attitude? Is he passionate about his service and his job?

Keep in mind that while you are interviewing your prospective lenders, they will also be interviewing you. They want to know if you are the type of client they can work with.

- Did you get all requested documents turned in promptly? Are you on time to appointments?
- Will you be available when needed to sign loan documents?
- Are you responsive when your lender calls you?
- Are you easy to work with?
- Do you have a good attitude?
- Can you adapt to changes in the loan program?
- Are you willing to cooperate and do your part?
- What is your communication style?

Since you will be interviewing each other, and discovering each other's working style, there will be lots of questions and answers. So take good notes!

Select 1 Lender to Serve You

After you have interviewed 3 lenders, talk with your spouse or the co-signer on your loan, and decide which lender to hire. Select 1 mortgage lender to serve you. Keep your second choice lender as a back up, a "Plan B" in case the first one does not work out. Then, call your favorite lender and congratulate him! Ask when you can meet to get qualified for your loan.

Non-Profit Organizations as Lenders

Another source of mortgage lending is a non-profit organization. Especially in metro areas, HUD-approved counseling agencies offer funding sources. Visit *www.NACA.com* to find out about a national non-profit agency called NACA (Neighborhood Assistance Corporation of America) which is a new program. They offer zero down payment loans for affordable home purchases.

All of these non-profit agencies have many restrictions, such as location of the home, income level, and debts. So be sure to research the programs first before you get excited about them. To get a loan, you will need to complete their home buyer education courses and meet their other qualifications. It can be quite a long process. Some agencies are government funded, and they stop lending when their funds are exhausted for the year.

Habitat for Humanity is a fabulous home buyer program that I highly recommend. However, their maximum income levels are so low that most buyers will not qualify. If you can get into their program, be prepared for a long wait list, and your family will be expected to contribute hundreds of hours building your home.

In some areas, you may find a self-help home building program. Peoples Self Help Housing has a wonderful program in San Luis Obispo, California. Of course, there are limitations. For example, the housing tract is already chosen for you, and it is usually a rural location. Again, you and your family will be required to help build your home.

Building your home can be a wonderful experience, because you obtain pride of ownership. Every time you look at your house, you will be reminded of the work you did with your own hands. And your family will take good care of the home for many years to come — because they helped build it, they have a vested interest in maintaining the good condition.

3. Give Docs to Lender

Which documents do you need to submit to your mortgage lender? At the minimum, you will need:

- 2 current pay stubs
- 2 current bank statements
- 2 current tax returns

Be prepared with your employer's name, address, and phone number of the human resources department. Your employer will verify your job.

In addition, you will need your landlord's name, address, and phone number. Your landlord will be asked to complete a form asking if you have paid your rent on time. Be prepared to show receipts or bank statements that prove you paid your rent for the last 12 to 24 months.

To meet the qualification requirements, your lender will ask you to provide documents. Remember that each borrower will have to meet all the requirements and provide all of their documents.

<u>TIP:</u> Every time you get a new paycheck or a new bank statement, you will need to provide these new documents to your lender during the home buying process.

2 Most Recent Paystubs (From Each Borrower)

If you are paid monthly or twice per month, 2 paycheck stubs are fine. However, if you are paid every 2 weeks, then you will need to provide 3 pay stubs. If you are paid every week, you will need 5 pay stubs. The reason is because you need to show a complete 30-day pay period.

If there is both a husband and a wife, you will need the last 30 days from both spouses. Each borrower who is signing on the loan will need pay stubs.

2 recent Bank Statements

You will need at least the last 2 months of your bank statement. Please copy ALL pages, even if the last page is blank. If you have more than 1 bank account, you will need 2 months of statements from each account. Even though you are qualified initially, as you continue this loan process, you will have to continue being qualified.

As you prepare to become a homeowner and get qualified, keep in mind that most lenders would prefer for you to have only 1 bank account. So if you have multiple bank accounts, eliminate those you are not using and consolidate down to only one bank account for your household. Of course that account may consist of both a savings and a checking account, but the goal is to have it all printed on 1 bank statement each month.

The only exception to this would be if you own a business or if you are an independent contractor. In that case, your tax preparer will advise you to keep a separate bank account for your business income and expenses. You do not want to co-mingle your personal funds and business funds.

Last 2 Tax Returns

Along with each tax return, you will need a copy of your W-2s from your employer and 1099's (if you are self-employed). You must submit a copy of every page of your tax returns. That means the Federal Tax Form 1040 and all attachments.

Self-employed Borrowers need P&L

If you are self-employed, you will need your business records too. That includes 1099's, a Profit and Loss Statement (P&L) and your business bank account statements. Your bookkeeper or accountant can help you prepare your profit and loss statements, which are commonly referred to as P&Ls.

Other Documents may be Requested

Additional documents that you may need to give to your lender include:

- Documentation showing other source of income (such as: child support, alimony, retirement, pension, social security, or disability). You may need an award letter, court records, or cancelled checks for the last 12 months.
- If you are receiving money as a gift to help with your down payment, you will need documentation of that income.

- You may need to provide copies of your credit card statements or your loan payments. That includes loans where you are the co-signer because you are responsible and it shows up on your credit report.

- You may need to bring copies of your utility bills.

- If you have had a divorce, your lender will need a copy of your final divorce decree from the court.

- If you previously filed for bankruptcy, had a short sale or a foreclosure, you will need to bring copies of the final documents.

- If you have deferred repayment of student loans, you should bring your deferral agreement as well.

- Finally, if you dispute any of your credit report items as listed on your credit report, and you can prove that it is wrong, please bring proof of that along to your lender. Your lender may be able to help you get it corrected on your credit report quickly.

4. Get Qualified

The first step to get pre-qualified for a mortgage loan is to complete a 1003 loan application.

Complete the Loan Application Form (1003)

Let's get pre-qualified! Now that you have found a great lender to work with, you are going to need to fill out the loan application form. It is called the **1003** (ten-oh-three) Freddie Mac form. The application is a 4-page form on legal size paper with lots of questions. You are going to write down your employment information for at least 2 years, your residences for the past 2 years, and list all outstanding loans and credit.

Remember that your credit report will be compared to this list, so make sure it is accurate. It will also ask you to list your assets, which are items of value that you own. Since you are a renter, your car is probably your biggest asset.

The form may look overwhelming at first, but do not get discouraged. Ask your lender if you can complete it online, which may help you tackle the form quicker, or perhaps your lender can complete it for you while asking you the questions. It's a great way to get it done quickly and easily.

We have included a blank 1003 in our sample document package so you can become familiar with this form.

Turn In to your Lender, Along with the Credit Check Fee

Now that you have completed the Form 1003, give it to your lender, along with the credit check fee. This fee can range from $7 per person to $35 per person, and some lenders will give a price break for married couples. This is because the credit bureaus combine reports for married couples so the reports may be less expensive for your lender to run. The credit report fee is non-refundable.

Some people may be nervous about having a lender run their credit report, but since you have already checked your credit, as we showed you, you feel confident about your report. In fact, you may even want to take a copy of your credit report into the lender. They will still have to run your credit report from their computer anyway, but it shows you are being proactive.

If you switch to another lender, your credit report will be pulled again. Having your credit report run so frequently can lower your credit score. This is one important reason why you want to shop for lenders **BEFORE** you select the best one. If you shop around for lenders at this point, and they each run your credit report, your credit score may get lower. So pick 1 great lender and stick with him!

Your Lender Calculates Loan amount, Monthly Payments, and Down Payment

The lender will show you what type of loan is best for you, what size of loan you qualify for, and how much cash you will need for your down payment. Using the credit report, along with your income documentation in the next step, your lender can now show you:

- What type of loan is best for you;
- How much you can afford to pay for a house; and
- How much money you will need for your down payment

Yes, even nothing down loans and VA borrowers need a cash down payment. You will need to write a check for an earnest money deposit when you make your offer to the seller. This is the check that will be deposited into an escrow account once the seller accepts your offer.

Your Loan Size Determines what Price Houses to Shop for

The less debt that shows up on your credit report means you will qualify for a higher loan and; therefore, be able to purchase a bigger, better house. Using your income and your expenses, your lender will calculate the maximum size of a loan for which you will be eligible. This will give you a good idea of the type of house for which you will be shopping.

Remember that your total monthly housing payment will include your mortgage payment, taxes, and insurance.

If you choose a condominium or planned unit development (PUD) that includes a monthly HOA payment, these fees will increase your housing payment. Then your mortgage payment will have to be less, which means that you will have to buy a lower priced condominium.

HOA fees are part of the payment when you live in a condominium or a PUD (which stands for a planned unit development). These are also known as common interest developments (CIDs). They are collected to maintain the private property in the community, such as streets, parks, swimming pool, building exteriors, yards, and other common areas.

For example, if your total housing debt allowed is $1,700 per month, and you find a condo that includes HOA dues of $300 per month, that only leaves $1,400 for your mortgage, taxes, and insurance.

5. Calculate Monthly Payment

At this point, your lender will crunch the numbers and give you some estimates. How much house can you afford, according to their calculations? Also, your lender will be providing a good faith estimate (GFE) form, which outlines the loan terms, the rate, and other important costs.

Ask Lender to Calculate your Total Monthly Payment

Your lender will calculate the maximum housing payment you can qualify for, which will include principal, interest, taxes, and insurance (PITI). Principal is the loan amount you borrowed that you are paying back and interest is the fee you pay for using that money. Property taxes are assessed and collected by your county government, and homeowners insurance is required by your lender to insure against fire damage.

What do PITI and HOA Stand for?

- PITI: Principal, Interest, Taxes, and Insurance
- HOA: Home Owners Association

Your monthly payment may also include homeowners' association fees, known as HOA fees, and any other expenses such as mortgage insurance, known as PMI, and Mello-Roos fees, which are common in California.

- Mortgage insurance, also known as private mortgage insurance (PMI), is required by some lenders when you do not have a large enough down payment. It helps to protect the lender by covering any losses they may incur if you default on your loan.
- In addition, some communities have additional recurring fees, such as the Mello-Roos tax, which is common in California housing tracts that were built in the last 20 years.

If your downpayment is less than 20% of the purchase price, you'll most likely have to pay monthly mortgage insurance. It's often referred to as "PMI" which is short for Private Mortgage Insurance. PMI protects the lender in case you default on your loan. PMI will increase your monthly payment, so you should avoid it if possible.

If you can't come up with enough down payment money to avoid PMI, then keep checking the property values later once you have more equity in your house. You may be able to get the PMI removed after you have 20% equity in your home.

The lender will calculate your housing ratio and your debt-to-income ratio. The PITI fees must be within your housing budget as determined by your lender.

You should be getting a fixed-rate loan. We do **NOT** recommend adjustable rate loans at all. Try to get the lowest interest rate possible. Remember that the lower the interest rate, the lower your payment, and the more house you can afford.

Calculate your Tax Return Deductions

Many homeowners receive deductions on their annual income tax returns from paying their mortgage interest payments. Although as I write this book, the MID (mortgage interest deduction) is in danger of being eliminated by our U.S. Congress.

Tax deductions are more complex and vary by your individual situation. It depends upon what tax bracket you are in and what itemized deductions you are already taking. As a renter, you were probably filing a 1040 or a 1040 EZ federal tax return. As a homeowner, you will have to file a 1040A tax return if you want to take the itemized deductions instead of the standard deductions.

Remember that your tax deduction will be calculated annually when you file your taxes, but you can divide that by 12 to find out how much savings you would be netting each month. Your accountant or tax preparer can give you estimated figures based upon your situation.

6. Pre-Approval Letter

Now it's time to get your approval letter in hand. If your lender accepts your documents, your credit score meets the requirements, and your debt ratios were calculated correctly, then let's get your approval letter. The 3 types of lender letters are pre-qualification, pre-approval, and approval.

Get a Pre-Approval Letter

A pre-approval letter is more valuable than a pre-qualified letter because it shows that your lender has analyzed your income, expenses, and credit.

Your lender will give you 3 types of loan letters:

1) A **pre-qualification letter** gives you and your RELATOR® the green light to start shopping for houses for sale. The letter includes the dollar amount for which you are qualified. It is an unofficial estimate and is not highly regarded for accuracy. The lender may not pull your credit or verify your income. Therefore, it does not take into account your entire financial picture, but it is a start and it is better than no letter at all.

2) A **pre-approval letter** is like a golden ticket. It shows how much money you can borrow and the interest rate of the loan. It is what allows you to make an offer on a house and receive serious consideration from the sellers. It's regarded as being much more credible, because the letter verifies that the lender has pulled your credit, verified your income, and analyzed your financial records. To get a pre-approval, most lenders will put your financial information into their computer and give you a desktop underwriting (DU) approval.

3) The third type of letter is an **approval letter**. It comes later in the process and it is specific to a home you are buying. It is a lender's commitment to loan you an exact amount of money, on a specific house, with a specific closing date. It will state the interest rate and your tentative payment amounts. Therefore, you cannot get the approval letter from your lender until you make an offer to purchase a home, and your offer is accepted by the sellers.

If You are NOT Qualified, What Can You Do?

If, on the other hand, you do not qualify, ask your lender what you can do to get qualified. You may need to reduce your debt, save more money, or improve your credit score. Perhaps you need to work at your job for a few more months.

Continue working on your credit and income to get yourself into a better financial position. If you keep working on it, a little bit every day, YES, you will be able to get approved.

Stay Focused on your Goal

If you do not qualify right now, don't be discouraged. Stay focused on your goal of home ownership and know it is going to happen soon. Just keep working toward your dream, a little bit every day. Be persistent and fight for your dream. Take one step every day and you will reach your goal before you know it.

7. Sign Buyer/Broker Representation Agreem

What is the value of signing a Buyer/Broker Representation Agreement?

- It is an employment agreement to hire your Realtor®
- You and your REALTOR® are committed to working with each other
- It allows your REALTOR® to write offers, submit offers, and negotiate on your behalf
- It allows your REALTOR® to receive compensation by working for you

With your Qualification Letter in Hand, Interview 3 REALTORS®

Now it is time to select a real estate agent to work for you. You have your choice of top real estate agents. There are so many real estate agents! So how do you choose the best one for you? Remember our formula: Research 5, interview 3, and select 1.

Find out about the business professional with whom you will be working closely. Is this a person you want representing you? Do you trust her to negotiate on your behalf? Find out his communication and working style. If you are tech savvy, you will be best suited by selecting an agent who also is tech savvy.

Find out each agent's reputation in the community. Can they provide you with recommendations from clients who have used their services? How much experience have they had with first-time homebuyers?

Why do I say that you should select a REALTOR® rather than just a plain real estate agent? A REALTOR® is a member of the National Association of REALTORS®; a licensed professional who has pledged to uphold a high standard of ethics. REALTORS® are also members of their state and local Association of REALTORS® and are accountable to their professional boards.

The REALTOR® Should Also Interview You

How will your agent know exactly what criteria you are seeking in a house? Remember that as you are interviewing your prospective agent, he is also interviewing you. They want to find out if your communication styles match and if you are a client they can work with successfully. Also, they will determine your qualifications and your commitment level to the home buying process.

Select 1 to Serve You

Sign a Buyer Broker Representation Agreement so the agent can begin working for you right away. A Buyer Broker Representation Agreement allows your agent to work on your behalf, to show you homes, to write and submit offers, and to negotiate those offers on your behalf. In most cases, you don't pay any money up front and there is no obligation if you do not purchase a home.

Your agent will need 100% cooperation from you as well. By signing a Buyer/Broker Representation Agreement, which is called a BRE in California and a BRA in other states, you are now obligated to work with your agent instead of other agents. A formal, written contract assures loyalty on both sides, and you can rest assured that your agent will be promoting your best interests.

Always hire the best team to work for you and represent you as the buyer! Your buyer's agent can represent you in purchasing a resale home, as well as new construction, HUD foreclosures and other REO bank-owned homes, and for sale by owner (FSBO) homes.

Here is one fabulous little perk about hiring a buyer's agent: In most states, including California, the seller typically pays for the buyer's agent. That is great news, as it means you will get a licensed professional to work for you, and someone else will pay her on your behalf! That is a great deal, if you ask me. You get a buyer's agent working with you, representing your interests exclusively and professional expertise on your side.

8. Include Decision-Makers

A decision-maker is anyone who will be financially invested, approving your decisions, or applying as a co-borrower on the loan with you. If your parents are gifting you money for a down payment, they are probably decision-makers who may want to be involved in the home search process. So be sure to keep them in the "loop" every step of the way.

Let your REALTOR® Know if Anyone Else must Approving your Home Purchase

If Mom or Dad are gifting you money for your down payment, I will bet they want to be involved in the house hunting, right? They want to see exactly what their son or daughter will be spending their hard-earned money on. That means EVERYONE will have to agree on the house together.

Are you Counting on Anyone Else's Financial Investment?

My motto is, *"No surprises"*, which means that you must plan ahead by anticipating others who will want to be part of the decision. Get everyone's blessings right up front. Does your co-borrower want to be involved with the entire process? On the other hand, do they just want to see the final home once you write an offer on it?

Some buyers have co-borrowers who help them qualify for the loan. You don't want to wait until the week before closing, and then all of a sudden, your co-borrowers withdraw their support because they do not agree with your decision. Next thing you know, your escrow is being cancelled, you have no house, and you have to forfeit your earnest money deposit.

Include Others in the Decision-Making Process from the Beginning

Do you have anyone helping you with the down payment or qualifying for the loan? Remember to tell your real estate agent right up front, that you will need to include these decision-makers in the process.

If you are a family of one (in other words, a single person) and you are purchasing solo, get advice and input from someone you trust. For example, your mom, dad, brother, sister, or best friend. Remember that while these folks are giving you advice, they do not have any legal obligations and your loan will be 100% in your name. YOU are the only final decision-maker.

Now, let's talk about your teenagers. It's important to get their support and commitment before the purchase of the home. Although they will not be co-signing on the loan, it is critical to have their cooperation when you move to a new neighborhood, especially if they have to change schools. Remember how teens are attached to their friends during high school and middle school.

TIP: Speak with your teenagers throughout the process. Explain each step, and ask for their feedback. Show them your final choice home and encourage them to become homeowners themselves one day.

9. New Listings on Market

How do you find out about the newest homes for sale as they come on the market? By receiving instant email alerts from your REALTOR®.

Register to Receive Email Alerts from your REALTOR®

How are you going to find homes for sale in your desired neighborhoods? The best way to preview homes is to sign up for an email alert system from your REALTOR®. Every time a new listing comes on the market, she will send you an instant automatic email. This email alert system is a great way to get a jump on your competition and view homes before other buyers are even aware of them. These are sent to you directly from the MLS database, so as soon as a listing agent puts the home listing in the computer, you will receive notification.

Receive New House Listings as Soon as They Come on the Market

You just need to tell your agent about your search criteria. Please specify the city, neighborhood or zip code, number of bedrooms, and your maximum price range.

If your search criteria are unrealistic — for example, you want a huge home in an upscale neighborhood for a rock-bottom price — you will receive very few email alerts, so you'll have to widen your criteria. On the other hand, if you get too many email alerts, then you should call your REALTOR® and narrow your search criteria.

Are You Already Receiving House Listings from a REALTOR®

If so, then she has already been providing you with a great service at no charge! If you are lucky enough to already have a REALTOR® who has kept you updated with the current listings, then you should strongly consider working with this real estate agent. After all, she has taken the time to help you get started in the hopes that you would become his client. Give this agent the first opportunity to be your real estate agent of choice by working exclusively with him.

Give that REALTOR® the First Opportunity to Serve You

Interview the REALTOR® and consider him as your first choice for your agent. He has already proven himself to you by working diligently on your behalf.

10. Drive by Selected Houses

Of course, you can talk to people, google information, and find data on wikipedia; but the BEST way to become familiar with the neighborhoods (and find the communities you like best) is to drive around and observe the neighborhood at various times of the day.

Select Homes from the Email List

From the email alert list, select homes as your neighborhood research homework. Now you are going to drive by the houses that you selected as your favorites. When you get the email list from your REALTOR®, choose some homes to view. Don't select more than 10, because that will be too many houses to compare and eliminate.

Drive by the Neighborhoods and Research the Communities

Before you view the inside of the house, first, you need to see if you like the home's setting. A property may look fantastic in a photo, but you never know what the neighborhood is like — until you go there in person.

Put your family in the car and drive by each home. Observe the neighborhoods and the communities. Talk about the features of each area. If you do not like the community, the neighbors, or the exterior of the house, then you can eliminate it from your list.

This process saves you a lot of time when you view homes with your real estate agent.

Become Familiar with the Geographic Areas you Prefer

Pick your favorite houses and learn about those neighborhoods. Do research online, attend community events there, stroll through the park and meet people. Ask questions of the residents who live in the area. What do they like best? Least?

Drive through the neighborhoods at various times of day, evening, and weekends. Visit the stores, schools, and churches in the area. What type of recreational facilities are available? Where do the children go after school? Do you feel safe? You should be able to get a good feel for the neighborhoods.

11. Property Types

Are you wondering what type of property would suit you best? Let's review the various types of home construction to clarify their differences. Remember there are regional variations in the terms used, so check with your real estate advisor.

Single Family Residence

A single family residence (SFR) is a detached stick-built free-standing home that is built as an individually owned home on its own lot (parcel). It does not share any walls with any other houses. Also called a "single-detached dwelling" or "detached home", the building is owned individually and occupied by 1 family unit. It usually includes an attached or detached garage. The property may also include a detached mother-in-law suite (granny unit) or a "casita" studio apartment.

A single family residence is the simplest type of home construction. Many home buyers prefer to have a separate, detached home. An SFR is the most expensive type of home category, but is the easiest type of house on which to get a mortgage loan.

CID / PUD

CID stands for Common Interest Development homes, referred to as PUD (Planned Unit Development) in some areas. Typically, homes are stick-built single-family or twin homes on their own lots. These homes are in planned neighborhoods with a Home Owners Association (HOA). They feature commonly-owned amenities such as a swimming pool, shared open spaces, or recreational facilities (for example, a tennis court). This private community may be gated.

A CID or PUD is often a detached home with a home owners association. In addition to any amenities such as a swimming pool, the HOA community may own roads and sidewalks. The HOA fees cover these common areas, but typically do not cover the home structures.

Condominium / Townhouse

What is a condominium? And what's the difference between a single family residence and a condo? A condominium is a home attached to other homes, in which each home owner owns ONLY their building, while the HOA owns and is responsible for the land, common areas, some exterior features of the buildings, and possibly the attached walls. The exact ownership is specified in the condo's CC&Rs and varies by condo complex. Condos may include garages, carports, parking spaces, or no parking rights at all.

Homeowners are said to own "airspace" within the boundaries of their house. They also share in the HOA ownership. With a condo, some insurance may already be included for the building structure, so find out what's included in the HOA before obtaining a quote from your insurance agent.

Condos often have smaller living space and less yard space than single family homes. That can be either a positive or a negative, depending on your housing goals. Condo owners love that they have very little yard space to maintain. But for families with school-age children, they may prefer to have a bigger back yard.

Benefits of condos:

Because of the common ownership, everyone contributes HOA fees, so prized amenities are available to all residents. For example, homeowners may have access to swimming pools, rec rooms, basketball courts, and BBQ facilities. Another benefit is that condos typically cost less than a free-standing home so they are perceived as more affordable. However, refer to the "Affordability" section below for more details.

Challenges of condos:

Common walls and small yards can reduce your privacy, and this can be a drawback. Living in close communities means that nosy neighbors may annoy each other, and there could be more friction. When the real estate market drops, condos are usually the first to depreciate because they don't maintain their value as well as detached homes.

Condos have HOAs, CC&Rs (Conditions, Covenants, and Restrictions), and additional rules which the residents must follow; their terms can be very restrictive. Another challenge with an HOA is that your neighbors are making and enforcing rules for the entire community. That can be either good or bad, depending on the experience level, effort, and attitude of your neighbors.

Mortgage Financing

Condos have restrictions which make financing more difficult than standard SFR homes. For buyers approved for FHA or VA loans, they can buy condos only in specific complexes which are pre-approved by FHA or VA. The complexes must have a certain owner-occupancy rate, a certain amount of HOA funds in reserve, and a certain percentage of the homeowners must be current on paying their HOA fees. Many condo complexes do not qualify or are not on the FHA or VA list.

First home buyers who are relying on FHA or VA financing will need to get a list of approved condo complexes in advance of house hunting. Your Realtor® should have access to the lists, and they are also available online. Refer to the internet links below:

- FHA approved condos: *https://entp.hud.gov/idapp/html/condlook.cfm*
- VA approved: *https://vip.vba.va.gov/portal/VBAH/VBAHome/condopudsearch*

Even with conventional financing, mortgage lenders will have certain restrictions for loaning money on condominiums. Verify the conditions with your preferred lender before you start shopping for homes.

Affordability

Perhaps you think you can't afford to buy an SFR house so you're shopping for condos because it seems that the payment will be lower. But with a condo, you're going to have to pay HOA fees, which can increase your monthly housing payment substantially. And remember that your lender will add the HOA fees to your debt ratios. So that means you will need higher income to qualify for a condo with HOA fees.

When deciding between a detached home and a condo, my advice is: Do the math. Calculate both scenarios and compare the difference. You might be surprised that a SFR may cost you the same monthly payment as a condo with HOA fees! Along with the fact that some condo complexes do not qualify for various types of financing, perhaps a detached home with no HOA fees is your best value.

Townhouses

Townhouses (or townhomes) are 2 or 3 story houses that share a common wall with the house next door. Townhouses are similar to row houses, except they are often divided into smaller groupings of homes, and hence they may be more desirable (and cost more). Refer to the next section, "Row Houses" for a comparison.

Row Houses or Attached Houses

A hallmark of East Coast housing, row homes are 3 or more houses built in a row that share common side walls with each other, but each home is individually owned. These charming old-style homes are built alike, giving the neighborhood a stylish look of uniformity that is still rich in character. Row homes are built on long, narrow lots and are renowned for their historic appeal in downtown metro areas. Typically each home has 2 stories, plus an attic and a basement.

Other names for row houses are row homes, terrace houses, patio houses, or townhouses. These side-by-side houses are referred to as "townhomes" in the Midwest, the South, and the Great Plains areas. Distinctive types of popular row houses are "brownstones" (New York) and "greystones" (Chicago).

In some neighborhoods, the term "row house" may refer to houses in which the side walls nearly touch each other, but are not shared "party" walls. For example, the famous "painted ladies" row houses in San Francisco do not share common walls but the side walls are only inches away from each other.

Twin Home or Semi-Detached

A twin home is a free standing home, except that it is attached to another home with a shared wall. Although they share a common wall, each home is on its own lot (parcel) and is individually owned. Twin homes are often located in CID or PUD communities (see above) and may include a monthly HOA fee.

Twin homes are also referred to as attached homes or semi-detached homes. They differ from a duplex (see below), because a twin home is 2 legal lots, separately owned; whereas a duplex is only 1 legal lot with 1 owner for the entire building.

Apartment Homes

With an apartment, you usually share a ceiling or floor with another residence; in other words, you have a neighbor living above you, below you, or both. In most of the U.S., the term "apartment" refers to a rented residence in a multi-unit complex of 5 or more units. However, in New York, apartment units are owned and purchased individually. This is unique to the East Coast housing market and a few other major metro cities. New York apartment ownership is similar to the condo ownership discussed above.

Multi-Unit Residences

A duplex is a 2-family home located on a single lot (parcel) and owned by one owner. Each residence has its own separate entrance. On the West Coast, a duplex is usually 2 houses side-by-side which are attached with a common wall. But in the Midwest, a duplex refers to a house with a residence on the main floor and a separate residence upstairs. A duplex is also known as a "two-family house". And a "flat" can refer to a residence within a multi-unit house.

A triplex has the same characteristics as a duplex, except that it consists of 3 units. It may also be referred to as a "three-family dwelling". A fourplex, also known as a quadplex or quadruplex, is a 4-unit building, also owned by 1 person but rented out to 4 separate families.

Most first home buyers will not be shopping for a multi-unit residence because the values are higher than a single family home, or because many duplexes/triplexes/quadruplexes are older homes in more dense neighborhoods.

And any building which has 5 or more units is typically considered commercial property; in other words, an apartment complex. These properties do not offer residential financing as they are designed for investors, not for owner-occupied home owners.

Manufactured Home

Mobile homes and manufactured homes are pre-fabricated houses (often called "coaches") that are manufactured off-site and hauled in to the site. What's the difference between a mobile home and a manufactured home? Typically a mobile home refers to a unit that was built before mid-1975, and is also known as a "pre-HUD" home. Manufactured homes, built after 1975, conform to a higher quality standard imposed by HUD.

Manufactured homes offer many benefits. Affordability is often a driving factor, because values are much lower than a single family home. It's wonderful that most mobile home parks include amenities such as a swimming pool, spa, clubhouse, and parks. Residents prefer manufactured homes over condos, because they want a home with NO common walls with neighbors. Senior parks often have planned activities and events which foster a strong sense of community.

The main drawback for manufactured homes is the lack of competitive financing rates and terms. So even though a mobile home may be priced lower than a detached stick-built home, it may be difficult or impossible for first home buyers to purchase. Older coaches were constructed with sub-standard processes (by today's standards), so there may be continual repairs and maintenance. Yard space is very minimal. Another challenge is the lack of garage space, as most coaches come standard with only a carport.

Mobile home parks are highly restrictive, so be sure to read their list of rules and regulations before you make an offer to purchase. Make an appointment to meet with the manager and bring your real estate advisor with you. Ask questions. Pet owners, for example, should ask: Are pets allowed? How many and what size? Do they have to stay indoors? Where can you walk them? Regarding residents, does every occupant need to apply and get approved by the management? How long can visitors stay? Can you rent out your home later on?

If you're thinking about a manufactured home, here are a few things to consider:

Senior or Family Park?

Some mobile home parks are specially designated for residents who are age 55 and better. The primary resident must be 55 years old, and other residents must adhere to the park's age policy for secondary residents. For example, many parks will allow secondary residents under 55 years old, as long as they are at least 35 (or 45) years old. Exceptions may be made for disabled residents and caretakers (with a doctor's note). The goal of a senior park is to cater to the needs of older adults, while excluding children and young people. Typically, senior parks are maintained well and valued higher than family parks.

If you have children, or if you're younger than 55, you'll need to look at homes in family parks. The quality of family parks vary. Some are extremely low quality neighborhoods, while others are very high quality neighborhoods. Choose carefully. Once you buy a mobile home, you should plan to live there for a long term. Manufactured homes are typically more difficult to sell than regular homes.

Leased Land or Rented Land?

Some manufactured home parks allow you to own the land (your lot) and other parks charge monthly rent for your lot. Manufactured homes on leased land are less expensive. They are less valuable because you only own your "coach" and not the land. You will have to pay monthly rent to the land owner. The rent may be limited by rent control, or it may be costly, depending on the specific mobile home park.

Manufactured homes on owned land, on the other hand, cost more because they include the land. Instead of paying rent, you will pay monthly HOA dues to the Home Owners

Association, which is much lower than rent would be. Resident-owned parks are often maintained to a higher standard, and the pride of ownership shows! Another great benefit of a mobile home on owned land is that you may receive better mortgage loan rates. So if you do buy a manufactured home, we recommend buying in a park with owned land.

Owned Land Type?

Resident-owned mobile home parks are usually structured as either a condo or coop. A condo ownership of a manufactured home lot is similar to the condo ownership explained above. In other words, each owner owns their own lot, and the HOA owns all the common land and the amenities.

A cooperative (coop) is a non-profit corporation which owns the entire land in the park and residents own shares in the corporation. The mobile home owners do NOT own their own lots. It is very difficult, if not impossible, to get financing for coop-owned mobile homes because the mortgage lender requires the coop to agree to be responsible, and often the coop board of directors will not assume that liability.

Mortgage Loans

As we discussed earlier, obtaining a mortgage loan on a mobile home can be challenging. Most lenders will want a higher downpayment than a regular stick-built home. Also the interest rate will be higher, and the term will be shorter, so your monthly loan payment may be almost as much as a regular house.

Many mobile home lenders will NOT loan on coaches that are single-wide, or on pre-HUD coaches built before 1975. If you are receiving an FHA or VA loan, it may require installation of a "permanent foundation" (known as 433A in California). And manufactured homes on rented land are less desirable.

Conclusion: research the parks and financing before you spend time viewing manufactured homes.

HOAs and CC&Rs

Condominiums and CIDs / PUDs typically have HOAs, CC&Rs, and additional rules that residents must follow.

CC&Rs stand for Conditions, Covenants, and Restrictions, which are formal rules that govern the homeowners. The CC&Rs are often filed in the public records with each property recording when the home is first built and sold. The new home developer is responsible for creating the CC&Rs and getting them approved before selling the house to the home buyer.

HOA stands for Home Owners Association. Each homeowner is a member of the HOA and is required to pay dues. HOA fees may include the cost to maintain the common areas, utilities, liability insurance, and staff salaries.

The members elect a Board of Directors to govern the HOA, and often hire a property manager to perform the daily management duties. The HOA board operates with bylaws, just like a regular corporation. The HOA creates and enforces rules for the residents; and of course homeowners are responsible for the behavior of their guests. The HOA sets the owner dues and has the legal power to collect the dues. In fact, some HOAs have the power to foreclose on a house if dues become delinquent.

HOAs provide a good service for their owners, but some people may consider their rules too restrictive. Get a copy of their rules in advance and read them through. Know what their regulations are BEFORE you purchase. We also recommend reading copies of the recent HOA newsletters and board meetings, which can be very revealing about what's really going on behind the scenes.

HOAs, especially smaller ones, may disband if many homeowners are delinquent in their HOA payments because the HOA does not have enough operating capital to survive. Once a condo complex loses their Home Owners Association, mortgage lenders probably will not loan on units in that complex. Which means the value of the entire condo complex will drop dramatically.

Before purchasing a home with an HOA, look around for signs of exterior building neglect — and read the HOA financial reports carefully. You need to do your research and ensure you are making a wise decision for your family.

Unique Properties: A Word of Caution

You may be considering buying a home that is not the typical first-home-buyer type of house. For example, you think you'll get a great deal when purchasing a foreclosure property, buying a fixer-upper, or by going direct to the seller. Perhaps your dream is to live on a ranch out in the country. Or maybe you're lured by the bright flags at new home developments.

Discuss your thoughts with your real estate agent and other advisors before pursuing one of these types of properties. Should you buy a fixer-upper? What about other unique homes? There may be pros and cons that you're not aware of. Let's discuss some of them now.

Fixer-Uppers Properties. Maybe while house-hunting, you find a house that is structurally and mechanically sound, but cosmetically is stuck in the year 1972. It still has green shag carpets and a pink bathtub, but you like the floor plan and you see the potential. You consider buying the house and then doing the improvements after you purchase it.

Why would buyers purchase a fixer-upper house; in other words, a house that is run-down and needs repairs? Often it's because home owners want to:

- Earn "sweat equity" by purchasing a fixer-upper home and doing the improvements themselves. They are trying to save money by purchasing a house with upside potential.
- Put their own personal decorating touch on the home, and re-design it to their custom standards. They want to do their own improvements.
- Enjoy doing projects. Some folks simply like DIY projects around the house.

While buying a "handyman special" sounds like a good concept, there are some challenges that make "fixers" NOT ideal for first home buyers. If you're interested in buying a fixer-upper, weigh the pros and cons thoroughly.

One problem is that some "fixer" homes with major structural issues will not qualify for mortgage loans, especially FHA or VA loans. That means you would have to pay all cash, unless you can qualify for a 203K or other construction loan.

Another challenge is that first home buyers often don't have enough cash on hand after close of escrow. Without a substantial sum, often $20,000 to $50,000, the work in the house never gets completed. Your family doesn't want to live in a half-finished house! Remember that you will pay for permits and hire licensed tradesmen, and the cost will probably be more than you anticipated. Also, when home owners haven't allotted enough money in their budget, they may try to cut corners. But shortcuts make the house worse instead of better.

One more challenge is the lack of home improvement skills. It's true that TV ads make you think you can easily "DIY" (Do It Yourself), but that can be misleading. During my real estate career, I saw many homes that depreciated in value due to DIY attempts. I've seen it all — substandard construction, faulty wiring, dangerous plumbing, leaky roofs, "glob-ons" (add-on rooms erected without permits and reflecting low quality construction), and poorly designed floor plans.

Lastly, where are you going to live while the remodeling is in progress? I advise you to stay in your old home until the work is completed... which costs you more in living expenses. So you'll need to account for overlapping occupancy of 2 months or more.

I understand that you may want a home with "upside potential" and that is a great reason to buy a fixer-upper. If you're insistent on purchasing a fixer, look for homes that need minor cosmetic improvements, such as paint, floors, and landscape. Do not take on a large-scale "fixer" home unless you are very experienced with house remodeling. Start small and learn as you go!

Bank Owned Property. Buying a foreclosure sounds like a great way to get a bargain priced home, doesn't it? And if you could buy a first-rate home at a low-end price, wouldn't everyone do that! Buying an REO (bank-owned property) is not as easy as you may think. There are not many bank-owned houses available for sale. The good ones get scooped up immediately (often by all-cash investors), and the houses left on the market often have problems: overpriced, poor condition, bad neighborhood, uncooperative agent, or uncooperative seller. Also, the title insurance may be a limited policy, with many exceptions compared to a non-REO property.

I believe it's important to work with a seller who cares about the quality of the home and about your family. Big banks are corporations. They do not care about you or your situation. They are not willing to be flexible and accommodate your needs. Big bank corporations are most concerned with their "bottom line". Therefore, I advise you to look for a house with a cooperative seller, and steer away from REO properties until you are more experienced with the home buying process.

For Sale By Owner. Known as FSBO properties, these homes are being sold directly by the seller without any representation from a licensed real estate agent. As a first home buyer, these homes generally will not be suitable for your situation. First off, the seller may not pay your agent a commission; therefore YOU would have to pay the entire commission out of your pocket. Secondly, unless the seller is highly sophisticated and experienced with the legal procedures, they may not supply you with the full coverage from disclosures, which an agent would typically prepare. Lastly, negotiations are very difficult without an agent representing each party, because emotions get in the way of logical business decisions.

Our recommendation: leave the FSBO's to the experienced buyers and investors!

Rural Home on Acreage. Living out in the country may seem like the ideal dream home. But rural property may not be a good choice for your first starter home. Land requires a lot of time and effort to maintain, and property upkeep can turn into a full-time job. Living "off the grid" is quite a challenging lifestyle because you are completely independent from standard utilities.

Unless you're familiar with country living, you may not be adequately prepared. Rural life might not meet your expectations. And once you buy a home, you can't "undo" it easily. Before you move to a new area, or make a major lifestyle change (like moving to a rural area), it would be best to try it out first by renting a rural home and make sure this new lifestyle suits you.

<u>**Brand New Homes.**</u> The new homes look so shiny and beautiful, don't they! Of course the model homes that you tour have upgraded features such as counters, flooring, and appliances, so the pricing can be surprisingly higher than you expect.

If you are considering purchasing a brand new home from a home developer, comparing prices with resale homes is like "apples & oranges". Resale homes can be negotiated **DOWN** in price. But brand new homes start with a "base price" and go **UP** (due to the upgrades). So new homes often cost more than you budgeted.

On resale homes, you can shop for houses priced higher than your budget, knowing that the sellers will usually negotiate lower. But on brand new homes, you will need to shop for a home price that is **LOWER** than your maximum budget, because upgrades will **INCREASE** your cost. Keep that in mind when shopping within your price range.

And of course, always visit new home developments WITH your real estate agent. Otherwise, your agent may not be able to represent you or to earn their pay for helping you.

<u>**Non-Traditional Construction.**</u> This category includes homes that do not meet the traditional construction types. For example, a geodesic dome constructed from a kit, a houseboat, or a mobile home with stick-built additions. Other non-traditional types of housing include coops (housing cooperatives) in which the homeowners only own a share in a corporation (not actual land), and leasehold condominiums built on leased (not owned) land.

Before pursuing houses built with non-traditional construction methods, check with your mortgage lender. Financing for a non-traditionally constructed home may be difficult or impossible.

You Are Now Ready to View the Inside of Homes that You Select

You've talked with your real estate advisor about the types of homes that suit you best. You've driven by the houses you like and narrowed down your list. You are now ready to view the inside of the homes that you liked from the outside. So let's continue on to "Step 3: Find a House". This is the exciting part!

STEP 3: Find A House

It is time to go house shopping! This is probably the most exciting part of buying a new home. Here is a preview of the steps.

1. Drive by houses
2. Select houses to view
3. Bring your checkbook and POF
4. View inside of homes
5. Take notes
6. Can you take photos?
7. Number your favorites
8. Narrow your choices to 1 house

First, we are going to drive by our favorite houses and narrow down our list. Then, we will select which houses we want to view with our REALTOR®.

Next, we will meet with our REALTOR® and bring our checkbook along, ready to make an offer. Our REALTOR® will show us the inside of the houses we already drove by and marked as our favorites.

We are going to take notes about the size of the house, the features, and write down any questions. We will snap a few photos, if allowed by the seller.

Then we'll all huddle together and discuss which houses we liked the best. We will number them in order, from best to least, and then narrow it down to just one favorite house.

See how quick and simple that can be? I have heard stories from buyers who took 3 months (or more) to find a house, and then another few months to close escrow. Finding your home and writing an offer should take only 1 day, if you do your research correctly ahead of time.

Follow our strategy and we'll show you exactly HOW to find your favorite house and write an offer on it, all in one day. What could be easier than that?

1. Drive by Houses

Once your real estate agent gives you a list of houses that match your search criteria, you should drive by the houses to view the neighborhoods before viewing the inside with your REALTOR®.

Set an Appointment with your REALTOR® to View Houses

Call your REALTOR® and tell her that you are ready to view the inside of homes. She will meet you at her office. Viewing homes will take approximately 5 hours. During that time, you should be able to view 5 to 7 homes and your goal is to make an offer on one home that day.

Since you have done your homework and you drove around and looked at neighborhoods, you should be familiar with various communities. Your REALTOR® has been sending you listings of houses as soon as they are put up for sale. Now that you have an appointment to meet with your REALTOR® and view homes, your challenge is to select only your favorite homes so you can view the insides.

Drive by the Fronts of the Houses.

Cross off your list any houses or neighborhoods you do not like. This is why you need to drive by the front of the homes **BEFORE** you view the insides with your REALTOR®. It will save you a lot of time later on. You will be really prepared and ready for your house-shopping appointment with your REALTOR®.

For example, if you have a list of 15 houses that you have seen photos online, you eliminated 5 and narrowed it down to your top 10. Then you drive by the houses and eliminate 3 more, which narrows down your list to your top 7 homes.

Start by eliminating those homes that you definitely do not want to view. Perhaps you don't like the neighborhood, or the street, or the style of the house. Remember that the house color and the landscaping can always be changed later, so be on the lookout for things that you cannot change after you buy it. By doing this footwork in advance, you will be truly prepared for viewing the interior of houses with your REALTOR®.

Everyone will be ready to go, and following this tip will help you speed up your offer. Get on the fast track to home ownership by doing your "homework" in advance!

Avoid Wasted Time by Pre-Selecting Homes

Select only the homes you really want to see with your REALTOR®. The challenge is NOT to waste your time viewing the inside of homes that you don't like from the outside. Your time is limited, and your time with your REALTOR® is even more limited.

Remember, your real estate agent has many clients to service and it takes a lot of time to show you houses. You want to use your time with your REALTOR® wisely. That is why you drive by first. The point of driving by the outside is to determine if you like the neighborhood and the exterior of the home. If not, it should be already crossed off your list.

One time I was showing houses to buyers. I had given them the same assignment that you have here, which is to drive by and view the exterior of each house. Well, it came down to house-hunting day. It had taken me a long time to coordinate the schedule with each seller so we could view the inside.

Each of the sellers was expecting us at a certain time, and the sellers left their houses so we could view the interior. As we drove up to one house, the buyers said, "This house is too ugly. We don't want to see the inside." I tried to convince them to view the interior, because the seller had gone to great pains to make the house available for them to view at that time. However, they refused to get out of the car and view the inside.

Obviously, they had not done their homework, which was to drive by the house first. It wasted our time — we only had time to view 5 houses and we could have viewed another house instead of this one. So everyone was a little bit uneasy about the situation.

Then, when the seller came home, he called me on my cell phone. The buyers were in the car with me. The seller said he did not see my business card on the counter, and he wanted to know why I never showed up to view the house. I explained that we drove to the house, but the buyers did not like the outside and therefore they did not want to go inside. The seller yelled at me for wasting his time, because he had specifically left his home for 2 hours so that we could view the house privately.

I could understand why he was upset and I had to apologize for my buyers. This was a little uncomfortable and put a wedge between my buyers and me. It was a big inconvenience to everyone, and a time-waster, as well as causing some negative feelings.

Learn from our mistakes and don't do this to your agent. If your agent gives you the addresses of the homes in advance, please drive by and make sure you like the exterior of the homes and the neighborhoods.

2. Select Houses to View

If you have 30 houses on your list, you should narrow it down to a handful that you really like. Then you can easily make a decision to purchase one of your favorite "finalists".

Did you know that a "green" home may cut your utility bill in half? When you think about the cost of water, electric, and fuel each month, all year long… you understand why it's important to search for homes with green or energy efficient features. Ask the seller for a BPI energy audit report or a HERS rating to verify your monthly energy cost, and to determine if rebates or savings are available to improving the home to higher energy efficient standards.

When selecting a home, think about your long-term usage. For example, your family may consist of a single person or a professional couple. So you may look at only 1 or 2 bedroom homes. But remember that your life situation will change in the future. Single people get married, and married couples have children. Allow room for expansion in the future.

For this reason, we advise you to consider a 3 bedroom home instead of 1 or 2 bedroom. Another reason to consider starting with a 3-bedroom is because of the higher resale value. There is less demand for 1 and 2 bedroom homes, as most buyers want at least a 3-bedroom, which will be easier to sell or rent. So we recommend that you consider future value when making your purchase decision.

Also keep in mind, **future resale value**. Lots of buyers are looking for turn-key ready homes with modern upgrades and home offices. So keep your wish list at the forefront, but also be aware of property values for the long term.

Select 5 to 7 Houses to View

Now you are going to select your favorite to view the interior. We recommend that you narrow it down to only a handful of houses. If you go out and look at 10 houses in one day, by the time you get to the last house, it will be difficult to remember the first house. That is why we say you should view five houses and make an offer on one.

Send this List to your REALTOR® 1 to 2 Days in Advance

From the list your REALTOR® has provided you, there are probably 20 or 30 homes on the list. You have selected your top 10, and then narrowed it down to seven or less. Let her know which ones you have selected so that she can set up the viewings.

Schedule to View Occupied Houses at Least 1 Day Ahead

Vacant homes can be shown at any time during daylight hours, as long as the listing agent has put an accessible lockbox on the house. Homes that are currently occupied by the sellers will need some advance notice so they can leave the house and you can view it privately. Houses that are occupied by tenants need at least 24 hours' notice, and sometimes more. You and your REALTOR® must always be respectful of the residents who live in a house, and must comply with the laws, too.

Remember, occupied houses may not have a lockbox, which means that your REALTOR® will have to coordinate a showing with the listing agent and/or the residents, and it will be more difficult to view the inside.

Why do you need to make sure you have plenty of daylight before viewing houses? Because it is difficult to really get a feel for a house unless you see it in full daylight. You will miss many of the features if it is dark. View homes during the daylight hours.

Vacant houses may have utilities turned off, which means daylight is the only light you will have. Even during daylight hours, some rooms may still be dark. Don't worry; your trusty REALTOR® will be prepared with a flashlight just in case.

Remember, in the winter it gets dark early so your home shopping time is limited. That means you may have to take a day off work to view homes.

Actually, weekdays are the best time to view a house anyway, because the seller's family is at work or at school during the day.

3. Bring Your Checkbook

When you meet your REALTOR®, you will need to bring 3 items with you to her office. Bring the following documents when you meet with your REALTOR® to start house shopping:

- An earnest money deposit check
- The pre-approval letter from your lender
- A bank statement (to show proof of funds)

We are going to discuss each item and its importance now.

Bring your Earnest Money Deposit Check to your REALTOR®'s Office

Now we are going to meet your REALTOR® at her office. Remember to take your check for the earnest money deposit, also known as EMD. Your REALTOR® will tell you how much to write it for, but it typically will be $1,000 or more. It depends upon the price of the houses you are viewing, and also upon the custom for your particular region. This will be your initial deposit on your offer to purchase a home.

In California, our buyers often make their check payable to "Escrow Company" since the buyer takes the check directly to escrow once their offer is accepted. We request that our buyer NOT write the name of a specific escrow company. It allows their REALTOR® to use a copy of your check again for another offer, just in case this offer is not accepted.

Give your REALTOR® a Copy of your EMD Check

Your REALTOR® needs a copy of this check for his files. He will cross out the confidential info at the bottom, which is your checking account number. Most agents will want you to hang onto the original check and they will keep a copy in their file.

In California, the buyer typically keeps their check until escrow is ready to open. We send the seller a copy of your check when you make your offer.

Even if you keep the original check in your checkbook, do NOT go out and spend the deposit. Make sure that your money for the deposit is ready and available at all times. You never know when your offer will be accepted!

Bring your Pre-Approval Letter from your Lender

You will also need to give your REALTOR® a copy of your pre-approval letter from your lender. This letter is like gold. It gives you access to view houses and to make offers. If you do not yet have a pre-approval letter, give him a copy of the pre-qualification letter instead. You will need this letter in order to make an offer to purchase your home today.

When your REALTOR® submits your offer, he will need to include a copy of this letter so the listing agent and the seller will know that you are qualified. If he does not have evidence that you are qualified, he may reject your offer and accept an offer from another buyer instead. It is to your benefit to ensure that you are competitive and you get the best shot possible when submitting your offer.

Bring a Copy of your Bank Statement as Proof of Funds

You will also need to bring a copy of a recent bank statement. In the real estate industry, it is known as Proof of Funds (POF). Your bank statement will show that you have enough money in your account to cover the check you wrote for the earnest money deposit, plus pay the balance of your down payment and any closing costs.

Even with a VA loan, a USDA loan, or a NACA "zero-down loan", you still need to put down an earnest money deposit and pay for some closing costs. By providing proof of funds, you are showing "good faith" that you are truly qualified for this purchase and you will be able to complete the transaction.

So get these 3 items together and bring them to your REALTOR®'s office. By providing this documentation, you are equipping your REALTOR® with the tools he needs to do his job. It gives your REALTOR® the confidence that you will be able to compete with other offers, and the knowledge that you will be able to close escrow when it is time to do so.

4. View Inside of Homes

When viewing the inside of houses, you should:

- Keep an open mind and be flexible
- Write down features, concerns, and questions
- Compare the houses to each other
- Realize that NO house will meet 100% of your "Wish List"

Teens may accompany you house hunting if they are well behaved. However, children under 12 years old will be bored with the house hunting, and it is not fair for them to be stuck driving around in a car all day. Once they get inside of a house, they will unleash all their energy, run around "playing" with items in the home, and possibly breaking things that you'll have to pay for... yikes! So get a sitter for the children in advance, or take them to Grandma's house. While you are busy house hunting, Grandma will enjoy her special time with the children.

You can still get the entire family involved in the home-buying process. Keep the kids updated on each step. Show them homes online and discuss the financial commitment.

After you select a final house and write an offer to purchase, you can take the children and show them the house. Then, they will get excited about their new bedrooms and the yard to play in.

Meet your REALTOR® to View Homes

Now you are ready to go shop for homes! Your REALTOR® will be prepared with a list of homes that you will be viewing today, including an MLS data sheet for each home. The data sheet includes the price, number of bedrooms, number of bathrooms, square footage of the house, year built, lot size, and monthly HOA dues. It will be handy to compare to each home as you view it.

Your REALTOR® will also provide you with a map of the homes you will be viewing today. She will have routed out the direction you will be taking. If you have a navigation system, bring it along, as it may come in handy.

View Homes with your REALTOR®

Your job now is to view and take in each house. To help you take notes and compare the houses, we have provided you with a House Comparison form in the appendix and on our website. Take this form with you and use it to help you narrow down to your favorite house at the end of the day.

At each home, your REALTOR® will point out good things, bad things, and interesting things. Remember that no house is perfect and every house has both good and bad features. This is your time for observing everything you can about each house.

Try to picture your furniture placed in the living room. Will this be a good kitchen in which to cook dinner? Do you know who will get each bedroom? Can you picture yourself barbecuing a steak on the grill in the back yard?

Keep an Open Mind!

Remember, there are things about the home you can easily change, and other things that are difficult to change, or cannot be changed at all. Try to overlook cosmetic things such as paint color, wallpaper, and carpeting. Most homeowners will want to add their own touch by redecorating anyway. Light fixtures, faucets, sinks, and counters can be easily changed. Even the "popcorn" ceiling can be removed.

Instead, focus on the structure, the design, and the layout of the house. These are things that cannot be changed easily, if at all.

In my ideal house, I do not want the kitchen to be visible from the entryway. Being a busy working mom, sometimes there are dirty dishes in the sink. I don't want to feel embarrassed if a guest comes in the front door and immediately sees our kitchen sink filled with dirty dishes. So I prefer floor plans that are open, but a kitchen hidden from the front door entry.

Another example is a family with babies or toddlers. They usually want to have the nursery right next to the master bedroom, so parents can get up to nurse the baby during the night. They feel safe and secure having the master bedroom near the children's bedrooms. On the other hand, families with teenagers usually want the children's rooms as far away from the parents as possible. Then the teens can play their music as loud as they want, without disturbing Mom and Dad.

Keep an open mind. You may be surprised that you end up loving the house you thought you wouldn't! You may feel unsure about a house and you may be thinking, "This is just not the right house for us." Then you go inside the home and start walking around, and get a good feel for the house.

Be Flexible. No House will Meet All your Needs and Wants 100%

So you have your wish list, right? All the things you want in a home, and all the things you DO NOT want. You are searching and looking for that perfect house. Well, I have a newsflash for you: The perfect house does not exist! I guarantee there is NO house that will meet your wish list 100% AND be in your budget.

> *"Wish lists and reality checks have another use. By prioritizing the items on your list, a good real estate agent can tell which items you might be willing to trade off... The bottom line: Unless you win the lottery or are independently wealthy, you're probably going to have to make some trade-offs when buying your first home." p.15 (Glink, 2000)*

Of course, if you are not happy with what your budget can buy you, then you may have to increase your budget and view houses in a higher price range. Even then, I can tell you from 25 years of experience, no house will be your perfect match. Not even a brand new house, unless you build your dream home from scratch and that's a huge life project we are not going to be discussing today.

5. Take Notes

Make notes of the following items at the houses you view. Look carefully at both the inside and the yard areas. Does the house include these items?

- Dishwasher
- Refrigerator
- Clothes washer and/or dryer
- Window coverings (blinds or built-ins)
- Light fixtures (such as a chandelier)
- Shed
- Workbench

Take a Notepad and Write Down the Pros and Cons of Each House

What notes should you be taking? Jot down what you like and do not like about each home. These notes will be invaluable when you are trying to make your purchase decision later. After a full day of house hunting, all the houses start to "run together" in your mind and you can easily forget which features each one had.

Make Notes of What is in the Home

Was there a dishwasher, refrigerator, washer or dryer, window coverings, light fixtures such as a chandelier, shed, workbench, or any other personal property?

To keep track of what's inside each home, write down which appliances are in the house, or any items of personal property that may be staying with the house. You will need to refer to this list later on when you write your offer to purchase. The MLS data sheet should list the personal property items that are (and are not) included in the purchase, but it is not always accurate. So it's best to do your own visual checklist.

What do you want included? The dishwasher or the micro-hood? What about the hot tub in the back yard, or the workbench in the garage? Don't automatically assume they are staying with the house. The clothes washer and dryer always seem to be a point of contention, so even if you ask for them in your offer, don't expect the seller to agree to leave them.

For example, you admire the beautiful blinds and the drapes and valance in the dining room that were custom-made for this house. You assume the sellers are leaving them behind, but the seller takes them and you are surprised after you purchase your new house and they are missing. Your REALTOR® will help you put everything in writing in your offer, even the little things.

On the other hand, what do you NOT want included in the purchase? For example, you may want an old rusty shed taken down, or a large satellite dish removed, or debris hauled away. Make a note so you can include this in your offer, too.

Write Down Obvious Defects with the Property and any Questions

If you see problems or defects, point these items out to your REALTOR®. If you have any questions, ask your agent. Keep in mind that she may not have the answers and she may have to ask the listing agent. So be sure to write down your questions or issues so they can be addressed later on.

> *"As you walk around the house on the second pass, inspect the paths, steps, patio, and driveway. The problems normally encountered with these items usually do not require immediate correction. Nevertheless, a tripping hazard might exist, cosmetic maintenance might be needed, or a condition might make the lower level vulnerable to water penetration. If you see problems in these areas, record them on your worksheet for early correction." p.36 (Becker, 2011)*

Remember you will have the opportunity to request that the seller repair things at their expense. That's another reason to write down any possible defects with the property.

6. Can You Take Photos?

Everyone has a camera or a video recorder on their mobile phone. People are taking pictures and video everywhere they go, so it just seems natural to want to take photos of a house you may purchase. But you should take photos of the homes only if you have written permission from the residents.

Is it Okay to Take Photos of Vacant Homes, if the Seller Agrees?

It is usually okay to take a photo of the house from the street because that is something the public can easily see. Besides, the photo of the front of the house is probably on Google maps already anyway.

However, to take photos of the interior, you should get permission from the seller. Even if it is a vacant house, the seller probably won't mind; but ask your REALTOR® to contact the seller and get permission first anyway.

However, do NOT Take Photos Inside Occupied Houses

Unless you have written permission from the residents, taking photos of occupied houses is a different story! Sellers and renters don't know you, and they don't know where you may distribute your photos. Many a surprise photo has been known to show up on Facebook, right?

A good rule of thumb is that if the house is occupied by sellers, get their permission, preferably in writing. If tenants live in the house, do not take photos. I know you want to take a photo so you can remember the house later on and it is so easy to pull out your cell phone and snap a picture, but remember this is not your home.

You should kindly refrain from photos or videos of a tenant-occupied house because you do not want to jeopardize the relationship between the tenants and the sellers. Instead, you will have to take good notes!

> *To document an owner's house, an owner requested that I take photos of the interior of his house that was occupied by tenants. When I went to the house, the husband said it was fine and I snapped a few photos for the owner. Then his wife came home! She was upset that photos of her prized collector plates might somehow get out. She did not want anyone to know about (or try to steal) her special plates.*
>
> *So she called me and requested that I bring the photos AND the negatives to her so she could destroy them. That was back before digital photos! It was a good lesson about how people value the privacy of their homes and their personal possessions. Even if something may seem trivial to you, remember how important it is to the person who lives there.*

If you DO take photos of a house, either the inside or the outside, do not distribute them to anyone. They are for your own personal use in deciding whether you want to purchase this home. The seller does not want to see photos or videos of their house landing on the internet or on YouTube! The seller would probably feel violated. Put yourself in their shoes and honor their privacy.

Always Be Respectful Inside a Homeowner's Personal Residence

Do not touch things, do not sit on their furniture, do not open their refrigerator, and do not peek inside drawers, cupboards, or medicine chests. Hopefully, you did not bring your children with you, but if you did, make sure they do not touch ANYTHING. It is nearly impossible for children to keep their hands to themselves. They just get so excited when they see new things, and cannot resist playing with them!

If the residents have cats or dogs, be aware of the family's wishes and be mindful not to let the pets go out of the house. Otherwise, you may be chasing that dog down the street and trying to corral him back into the house. Use the restroom before you leave the office to view houses, so you won't have to use the restroom at a seller's home while viewing it — or worse, at a vacant house without tissue paper!

If you opened doors or windows, please shut them. Be sure to lock up any door you may have unlocked before you leave. The residents have placed a lot of faith in you and your REALTOR® and they trust that you would treat their private home with courtesy. Just as you would not want someone to violate your personal space, be respectful of their homes also.

7. Number Your Favorites

Your "winners" list will include houses that are in good condition, fit your price range, and meet 85% of your "wish list" criteria:

Number the Houses You Liked the Most (1, 2, 3)

Now that you've spent an entire day house hunting, or maybe even a couple of weekends, it's time for you and your wife or husband to discuss which house you're going to write an offer on. What are the pros and cons about each house? Which do you like better than the others? If you cannot agree on your top choices, can you agree on which ones you would like to eliminate? Then, you are left with your favorites. Rank them in order from best to least favorite.

Remember that NO House is Going to Meet ALL of your Criteria

No home will meet ALL of your "wants and needs" on your wish list. If you are shopping in the lower price ranges, those homes will have upgrades. If you are selecting from houses within your budget range and you do not like what they have to offer, you may need to either increase your budget, or be willing to give in on some of your wish list items.

Once I was watching a TV show about houses being sold for several millions of dollars. The buyer had a budget of $2M (two million dollars). She was looking at expensive, gorgeous homes and she did not want to buy any of them.

None of them had ALL the features that she desired. Her real estate agent advised her that in order to get all the features on her wish list, she was going to have to buy a house in the three-million-dollar range! He advised her either to be flexible with her wish list, or to increase her budget. Now, most of us are not on a 2 million dollar budget but we still can benefit from his smart advice.

If a House Meets 85% of your Criteria, Put it on Your List

If it is in good condition, and fits your price range, then it is a winner. The bottom line is, regardless of what price range you are shopping in, you will not find a home that meets 100% of your wants. Prioritize your needs and wants. That is why you are taking notes, to help you select the BEST choice.

My rule of thumb is if you find a house that meets 85% of your wish list, it is a serious contender. Make an offer to purchase it. Do not let this opportunity pass by you.

Remember you are going to customize your home after you move in and make it uniquely yours. So if you like the structure, the layout, and the design, put this house on your "winners" list.

This is Yust your STARTER home — You Can Trade Up to your DREAM Home Later!

You can do many things to make your new house unique and suited to your family. You can paint, put in new flooring, and landscape the yard. You can upgrade the light fixtures, faucets, and counters. You can decorate your new home with your own style and flair. Instead of looking at what you cannot buy, think about what you can buy, and what you can do with it.

You may not qualify for the large luxury house, but whatever you do buy, will be all yours! Once you are in the house for a few years, hopefully you will have earned some equity. Then you can use your equity and trade up to a bigger house. The important thing is to get started by purchasing a home today.

Perhaps you feel that if you compromise, you won't get your dream home. Actually, any home you buy today is a dream home because you are no longer a renter; you are fulfilling the American Dream of home ownership!

8. Narrow to One House

Wow, that is hard! You saw so many homes you loved, how do you narrow down your list to your #1 top choice? Here are a few tips:

- Review your notes
- Compare the features of each house
- Consider the style and design you like best
- Talk with each other and your Realtor®
- Figure out how much fix-up work or re-decorating you will need to do
- Calculate the value you get for the size
- Think about how your family will use the floor plan

Narrow it Down to Just 1 Home, but Keep 2 Homes as Back-Ups

As you have already been going through the process of discussing the houses, and ranking them from best to least favorite, you have probably narrowed it down to your top 3 choices. We are going to select 1 as our top favorite, but we are going to keep the second and third favorites as our "Plan B" and "Plan C" just in case.

Why is that? We don't always get our first choice of house. We may find out that the sellers have already accepted another offer, or they decided to take the home off the market. Maybe our lender will not approve that house. Perhaps we find out there are too many repairs and the house would not work for us. Maybe the sellers would not agree to our price and terms. Then we will have to move on to your second and third choices.

Make a List of Questions and Concerns About your #1 Home

Start with your #1 house and make a list. Go through your notes and talk with your REALTOR® about your questions and concerns. What appliances were in the house? Were there things that need to be repaired? Is there a copy of a previous home inspection you can view?

Your REALTOR® Can Take you Back to View your Top Choices Again

Now we have got our favorite houses picked out. If you really cannot decide between your two top choices, your REALTOR® can take you back to those 2 houses again. Viewing each of them carefully should help you identify your top choice home.

Do Not Get Emotionally Attached to Houses Yet

Remember, this is just the starting point for your home purchase. You may or may not get this house. Although it is your #1 pick, don't get too excited. We are still in the initial phase. If it turns out this house does not work out for you, you do not want to be too disappointed.

> *"Intangible benefits, such as peace of mind, pride of ownership and security are important; they should be part of a homeownership decision, but don't let emotions overrule a rational decision." (Nielsen, 2009)*

Ride the momentum and get ready to start your offer! You are taking action and you are on the way to your dream of home ownership.

STEP 4: Write Your Offer

Now it is time to write up your offer. You are going back to your REALTOR'S® office and together you will decide what purchase price to offer. Go back to the office.

1. Discuss the price and terms of your offer
2. Call the listing agent
3. View neighborhood comps
4. Write an offer
5. Prepare for inspections and negotiate the home warranty
6. Sign the purchase offer

Your REALTOR® will call the listing agent and ask him all of the questions on your list. Then she will pull up recent sales in the neighborhood to show you the value of the house on which you will write an offer. She will write up your offer, and include important things like inspections and your home warranty. Lastly, you are going to sign your purchase offer to buy your first home!

1. Go Back to the Office

Once you have viewed homes with your REALTOR®, you will all go back to the office to discuss which property you want to buy. Let's get started!

Return to REALTOR®'s Office to Write your Offer

Okay, so now you are going back to your REALTOR®'s office and it is time to write your offer! However, the office may be a long distance away, so you may stop at a coffee shop or diner instead. Besides, all this house hunting has made everyone hungry so maybe you'll get a bite to eat while writing up your offer.

Instead of stopping at the office, you can just go back to your top #1 property if it is vacant, and write the offer there. It's a great feeling to be sitting inside your new home while you write the offer on it; and, while you are there, you may see appliances or items that you need to include in your offer. It may also trigger additional questions. However, remember that a vacant house will have NO table, NO chairs, and maybe even NO electricity (which means no light after sunset).

Your REALTOR® Can Write and Sign the Offer "On the Spot" with Her Mobile Office

If you are working with a top real estate advisor who has a mobile office, including a laptop computer, a tablet, or an iPad, he can simply write your offer immediately and you can sign it on the spot. With mobile internet, your REALTOR® has access to all the forms needed to write an offer. She can even go through it with you and explain it as they complete the purchase offer.

2. Discuss the Price and Terms of the Offer

Now it is time to talk about what is going to be in your purchase contract. Every contract has 2 parts: The first part is the price, and the second part is the terms, which is everything else besides the price. So remember that price is only PART of the offer. When you and the seller don't agree on price, you can always change the terms to get them to agree to your price. And they can always give you "concessions" such as a credit (money allowance) for the closing costs. Remember, it's all negotiable!

> *"Negotiating is the process of getting someone to do something, even if they disagree with it, by giving them enough concessions to make it worth their while." p.30 (Thomas, 2005)*

Discuss the Following with your REALTOR®:

- What price do you think is fair?
- Which appliances or personal property do you want to include in your offer?
- How soon do you want to close escrow?
- Which title or escrow/settlement company do you prefer?
- Any questions you may have about the property

What Price Do You Think is Fair?

Discuss now with your REALTOR®, what price you think is fair. You want to make sure that you are going to get a good deal on the price, so you do not want to offer more than you have to. On the other hand, there may be competing offers from other buyers, so you want your price to be high enough to beat out the other buyers. We will discuss the importance of comparing other similar properties.

Now, you want facts AND an honest opinion. This is where your REALTOR® can shine as your trusted advisor and consultant. Ask him for an opinion. How much would your real estate advisor offer for this house, if he were in your shoes? Yes, your REALTOR® is going to run a comparable market analysis (CMA), show you the comps, and help you crunch the numbers. However, it all comes down to "gut feeling" sometimes, and you have to feel good about your purchase.

As we mentioned in the beginning, never make a "low-ball" offer. I know you are trying to get a bargain, but that is not the right way to go about it. An unreasonably low offer will only offend the seller and then you definitely will **NOT** get your house!

Which Appliances or Personal Property Do You Want with the Home?

Pull out your notes and the MLS data sheet. Which appliances were in the house? Verify it includes the stove, oven, refrigerator, dishwasher, micro-hood, clothes washer, or dryer. What does the data sheet say about the appliances? Are they built-in, slide-in, or portable? Do you want to keep them in the house? Be sure to ask for the appliances you want, but realize that the sellers may want to take some with them — usually the clothes washer and dryer, and often times the refrigerator.

Earlier we discussed other negotiable items of personal property, such as the chandelier or other light fixtures, window coverings, portable shed, workbench, hot tub, and satellite dish. If you want it, put it in your offer. If you want it removed, make sure to put that in the offer, too.

In most cases, the "inside" window coverings (such as blinds or shades) will stay, while the "decorative" window coverings (such as drapes and valances) will be leaving with the seller. Never assume! It is always a good idea to put it in writing so there are clear expectations on both sides and no one is disappointed later.

How Soon Do You Want to Close Escrow?

Most buyers prefer to close within a month or so, and a typical escrow closing period is 30 days. However, for buyers who are receiving a government loan such as FHA, VA, or USDA, they can expect a slightly longer escrow, which may be 60 days or more. If you are buying a short sale, the escrow period is usually 3 to 6 months. If you have a complex loan, are buying an REO, or there are other delays, always plan an extra few weeks just in case.

Sometimes the sellers do not want to move out until the school year is over, so their children can change schools during summer break. Therefore, it's common for a seller to request the escrow closing date be timed to coincide with the end of the school year. Or perhaps they are relocating to another state and want their new home purchase to close escrow simultaneous with this sale.

Which Title or Escrow Company Do You Prefer?

Do you have a specific title or escrow/settlement company that you prefer to use? If so, be sure to let your REALTOR® know. Most buyers will defer to their agent's recommendation of an escrow company with whom she has developed a good working relationship. In some states, the escrow/settlement company is known as a settlement company. In other states, an attorney's office handles all the closing funds and paperwork, instead of an escrow/settlement company.

Your REALTOR® may recommend that you use the seller's choice of escrow/settlement and title company. The seller may have already started a file at an escrow company; for example, if the property has already been in escrow with another buyer. If it is a short sale, then chances are that they have already been working with an escrow company they would prefer to continue using. If you are buying a brand new house from a developer, the seller will require you to use their escrow company because they have already negotiated a contract with them. If the property is an REO, meaning that it is owned by a bank, then the buyer is obligated to use the bank's preferred escrow company.

This is where you will look to your REALTOR® for advice. He is experienced in dealing with these issues and will be able to write up the contract in the manner that is best for you, your agent will ensure that your offer is as competitive as possible.

If you want to view a list of each state and their typical closing procedures, take a look at the "State-by-State Guide to Real Estate Closing Practices in the U.S." which is Appendix B in Gadow's book, *The Complete Guide to Your Real Estate Closing: Answers to All Your Questions - From Opening Escrow, to Negotiating Fees, to Signing the Closing Papers.* This list is an excellent reference if you are unfamiliar with your state's legal and customary procedures for closing.

Ask any Questions You May Have About the Property

Now take out your notes, review them, and ask any questions that you have about the house. Express your specific concerns to your REALTOR®. Now you see why it was so beneficial to take notes earlier! Your agent will make sure to find out the answers to your questions.

3. Call the Listing Agent

Your REALTOR® will contact the seller's agent to ask questions about the home. You should never contact the other agent or the seller directly. After all, that is why you hired an agent — to do the negotiating for you!

Your REALTOR® Calls the Listing Agent of the Home You Selected

To start the process of developing good communication with the seller's agent, your REALTOR® will call the listing agent to ask questions and find out how to ensure your offer will be competitive and accepted right away. This is a great example of how your agent works hard to develop good business relationships that benefit you.

In Speaker-Phone Mode, You Can All Listen to the Listing Agent

Your REALTOR® will put her phone into speakerphone mode, so you can all listen together. She will let the seller's agent know which house she's calling about, and that you, the buyers, are listening also. It gives you the opportunity to hear what the seller's agent says. I recommend that you allow your agent to do the talking and direct the conversation. She already knows what your questions are because you have just discussed them with her.

Let Your Agent Ask the Questions

Your REALTOR® will discuss with the other REALTOR® the price, terms, escrow and title company preference, inspections and reports available, vendors, and closing date. He will ask if there are any reports available, such as a termite report or a home inspection report.

Additionally, he will find out if the sellers have received any other offers. Your REALTOR® will ask how the listing agent prefers to receive the offer, and the expected response time to your offer. This conversation gives you the opportunity to find out more about the home and the transaction, and to be a part of the discussion as it unfolds.

Your REALTOR® will have the opportunity to ask your questions and find out answers. Some of your questions may be, for example: When was the new roof put on? If you noticed ceiling stains, have they had any leaks? Was the fireplace cleaned recently? Does the hot tub work? Do they plan to leave the washer and dryer? Did they get a building permit when they added on the family room? How soon will the residents be moving out? You did not see an air conditioner, so what type of cooling system is there? If the garage door appears to be broken, does it work properly?

Your REALTOR® will want to ask other logistical questions, such as the name of the seller's lender (if it is a short sale), the additional documents needed (if it is an REO), and the status of any previous offers that were canceled. This phone conversation is a great way to establish a good working rapport between agents, and it gives you a competitive edge on your offer.

Now that you know the details about the property, and you are aware of what the seller is looking for, you can structure your offer accordingly. This knowledge will put you miles ahead of other buyers who send in "blind" offers!

4. View Neighborhood Comps

Homes that are in a similar neighborhood, are similar sizes, and were built around the same time period, are called "comparable" because they can be compared to each other. Comparable properties are those that recently sold in the same region. In the real estate industry, we use the term "comps" for short.

Your REALTOR® Shows You Comps

The last thing you want to do before writing an offer is to find out data about homes that just sold in this neighborhood. Although you and your REALTOR® have a price in mind, based on what you think the fair market value is and your gut feeling, it is always reassuring to see it in writing and know that you are getting a good deal.

Your REALTOR® will pull up a list of houses that have sold recently in this neighborhood. The list is called a comparable market analysis (CMA) and it includes the final sale price, the square feet, year built, bedrooms, and bathrooms, for each home.

A CMA would include the following facts:

- Which properties sold recently
- Distance to the subject property
- Average price per square foot of sold properties
- Average percentage of list price to sold price
- Average number of days on the market

Analyze the Comps to Write a Fair Offer

You can now compare these similar homes to the one on which you are making an offer to purchase. Remember that no 2 houses are identical — even if they are in the same tract and have the same floor plan. Some homes were better maintained over the years, and even upgraded. Some houses have amenities, such as a swimming pool, which may (or may not) increase the value. By comparing these houses to your new house, you will get a good feel for value.

Decide on a price range you are willing to pay for this house. Determine your lowest and highest price. Your lowest price may be your starting offer. Set an upper boundary so that you will not be caught up in the bidding frenzy and overpay for the house.

The comps will let you know that you are in the "ballpark". Remember, there is no "right" or "wrong" price.

Consider Making your Offer Slightly Lower so You Have Negotiating Room

Just because it is listed for sale at a certain price, does not mean that's the price you are going to offer. A listing price does not mean that is what the house is worth. Remember, the value of a house is determined by what qualified buyers are willing to pay, what the sellers will agree to accept, and the valuation as determined by your mortgage lender's appraiser.

After you and your real estate advisor determine the home's value, write your offer slightly lower than the actual value. There's a little margin built into the price that the sellers are asking, but we do not want to be too high or too low. You want to get a great bargain, but at the same time, your price must be high enough to beat out other buyers and be accepted by the seller. You want to know that your offer is a fair price for everyone.

If your offer is the only offer in sight, your REALTOR® may advise you to offer slightly below the asking price. Remember that if it is substantially below the asking price, the sellers will probably come back with a counter offer. If the sellers accept your first offer, you won't have to go through many negotiations, and there will not be an opportunity for other buyers to get their offers in before yours gets accepted. So you want your offer to be accepted right away the first time, and you will need to be as competitive as possible.

> When my buyer clients submit an offer, we look at the percentage the comps sold for, as compared to what they were asking.
>
> For example, if the comps sold for an average of 96% of their list price, we know the sellers went down about 4%. So we might consider making a starting offer of 6% or 7% below the list price, knowing that the seller may counter back up to 4% or 5% off.

In a Competitive Bidding Situation, Begin with your "Highest and Best" Offer

On properties where there are many buyers bidding, you may want to start with your highest offer instead of your lowest offer. Your agent will gauge the level of competition to determine the offer pricing.

Caution: just because a listing agent says "submit your highest and best offer" does not necessarily mean there are multiple buyers, or that you have to start with your highest price. Often the term "highest and best" is used as a marketing strategy by the listing agent to give the appearance of a property in high demand.

Remember that price is only a part of your offer. The other part of your offer is terms and maybe instead of a lower price, you want the seller to give you some concessions, such as paying part of your closing costs.

Negotiating tip: always emphasize the benefit to the seller, and how he can "win" with your offer. For example: "We are willing to delay the close of escrow until June, so your children can finish the school year in your current house."

5. Write an Offer

The most important concept to keep in mind when writing your purchase offer is: *Everything is always negotiable between the buyer and the seller*. However, after you both come to an agreement in writing, the negotiating stops and you must adhere to your written agreement. A purchase offer may also be referred to as a "bid", depending on the region.

Make an Offer to Purchase your Favorite Home

Now it is time to write your offer! This is where pen comes to paper, (or in some cases, stylus comes to iPad), to put the transaction together. So today, right now, your REALTOR® will write an offer for the purchase of your first home. All you have to do is sign it!

Review a Property Profile to get the Legal Information

A property profile is a report that is pulled from the county tax records. It shows the owner's legal name and status. Do not assume that the sellers own the property in their names. The property may actually be in a family trust, or you may be surprised to find out that only the wife's name is on title because her husband quit-claimed his interest to her. That is why your REALTOR® will always check the tax records before typing up the offer to purchase.

The records will show the legal data, such as number of bedrooms, square feet, lot size and structure type. Other important information on the report will include the name of the mortgage company, the amount of money borrowed on the loan, and date of the mortgage. The mortgage information can help your agent determine whether it is a short sale or an equity sale.

Your REALTOR® Completes the Purchase Offer

The purchase offer (sales contract), includes the sale price, deposit amount, mortgage financing, other terms, and any contingencies. In California, our standard offer form from the California Association of REALTORS® is called a Residential Purchase Agreement and Joint Escrow Instructions, or RPA-CA for short. It serves as the purchase offer, the purchase contract (along with any counter offers), and the escrow instructions. It is like 3 forms in 1.

Ask your agent about any "contingencies" or "subject to's". It means those items must be satisfied before the contract can be fully consummated. Until all of the contingencies are met, you can typically back out without penalty.

Which Party is Responsible for Paying what Closing Costs?

Closing costs and inspection fees and reports will need to be paid. Which party will pay for each cost? The purchase includes escrow or attorney fees, title insurance for the seller, pest control inspection, septic or well testing, natural hazard zone disclosure report, smoke detector installation and government compliance, county and city transfer tax, private transfer fees, HOA transfer fees and document preparation fees, and, of course, don't forget your home warranty.

Although certain expenses are customarily split a certain way in your region, they are not "set in stone". It is your offer and you can offer whatever you like. You can ask the seller to pay for things that are typically paid by the buyer. There is nothing wrong with requesting it! Remember: in business, everything is negotiable.

You can also request that the seller pay part of your closing costs. Your REALTOR® will help you ask for the right amount. If you are paying all cash, however, do not expect to get a credit for closing costs.

Your offer may or may not be accepted. Keep in mind that it is a process. There may be negotiations, or you may decide to move on to another house instead. Whatever happens with this offer, I guarantee that you WILL get the right house at the right time and I promise you will LOVE your new home once you move in and make it all yours!

6. Prepare for Inspection and Negotiate the Home Warranty

The following items are important and should be included with your home purchase:

- Pest control report
- Home inspection report (aka structural building or physical inspection)
- Home warranty

Always Order a Home Building Inspection!

Would you ever buy a used car without having your mechanic inspect it, test it, and check it out completely? No, you would get it inspected by your trusted mechanic, because you want to ensure that your car is in good condition before you pay for it and drive it off the car lot.

Well, your house is an even bigger investment than a car, is it not? Naturally, before you commit to a purchase that is hundreds of thousands of dollars, you want to know your new home's structural condition.

Your REALTOR® will recommend ordering a professional home inspection from a reputable company. In some states, home inspectors are licensed by the state, but there is no licensing required in California.

How do you know if you're hiring a top notch professional you can trust? Always ask if the home inspector is a member of the California Real Estate Inspection Association (CREIA), American Society of Home Inspectors (ASHI), National Association of Home Inspectors (NAHI), or International Association of Certified Home Inspectors (InterNACHI).

Search the web sites of these associations to find home inspectors in your area who belong to professional organizations. They are required to attend continuing education, comply with state regulations, follow standards of practice, and uphold a code of ethics.

Many top inspectors write blogs with advice for homebuyers. Search online at *www.ActiveRain.com* and check out blogs of home inspectors in your area. How well do they know their trade? What are clients saying about them? How are they rated, and what recommendations have they received?

My criteria for selecting a quality home inspector would be:

- Recommendation from REALTOR® and past clients
- Communication style and accessibility
- Type of report produced
- Color photos included
- Promptness in completing inspection
- Turn-around time of report
- Ability to deliver the report electronically

Before the home inspection, your REALTOR® will work with the seller's agent to make sure that the utilities are turned on. The water, power, and fuel need to be turned on so your inspector can test the plumbing, the electricity, and the furnace.

Once I represented a client who was buying a house. The seller's real estate agent knew the home inspection was scheduled, but did not get the gas turned on before the inspection. The home inspector, therefore, was not able to check the working condition of the furnace, and he noted that on his report.

After the buyer purchased the house and moved in, she found out that the furnace was broken! It was not covered under the home warranty repair because it had been broken prior to the close of escrow. The seller had not disclosed the broken furnace as they should have. The buyer had the furnace repaired and sent the bill to the seller, and, fortunately, they did the right thing and paid the bill.

Not every situation may work out with a good ending. A method to prevent issues from occurring is to make sure the utilities are turned on before the home inspection.

You really want to see the home inspector in action, don't you? This is exciting and you are anxious to find out everything about your new home.

However, during the home inspection, the inspector will not want you leaning over his shoulder watching everything he does. The inspection is about 3 hours, and that is quite a long time for the inspector to work with someone following him around.

Instead of watching his every move, I suggest meeting the inspector toward the end of the inspection. That way he can perform his work quickly and quietly, and then when you show up, he will give you a hands-on demo of the problems he found. You can make note of the major issues, but remember the inspector already took photos of the problem areas and they will be noted on his report.

A few days after the home inspection, you will receive the home inspection report. It will be quite extensive, about 20 to 30 pages long. If it is any shorter than that, I might be worried that it was not thorough enough.

We have included a sample report in the appendix (and on our website) for your convenience. The report has several different sections, including items that are critical and must be fixed immediately. Verify if any items are "health and safety" repairs. Check those items first and determine what needs to be fixed before you purchase the house.

Review the report with your REALTOR® and ask any questions. He will help you determine what you should ask the seller to fix, or if you should ask the seller for a credit and then fix it yourself. If you agree, your REALTOR® will prepare a Repair Request form to give to the sellers.

Remember that the seller is typically selling the house "as is" except for mandatory government compliance, and they are NOT obligated to fix anything. "As is" means nothing will be fixed or changed. However, the sellers are still obligated to disclose all known defects and problems.

One last tip about home inspections: Keep in mind that NO home is perfect, not even a brand new home. So the question is, "should you get an inspection of a brand-new home?"

My answer is always **YES**. Protect yourself and know what is behind the walls in your home **BEFORE**, not AFTER, you purchase it. It doesn't have to be perfect. You just need to know its condition.

Get a Termite Inspection, and Any Other Inspections Needed

You will probably also need a pest control inspection, as your lender often requires it. Termites are small bugs that live in the timbers of your house and eat the wood. You may see some of their droppings along windowsills. Termites and other pests are more frequent in areas with high humidity.

A pest control inspection is also known as a termite inspection, although the inspector will also be checking for rotten wood, water damage, water intrusion, and signs of mold.

How do you select a good pest control inspector? The same way you select a home inspector. Your agent may recommend several inspectors with good reputations and solid track records. In California, and most states, pest control inspectors must be licensed.

On a pest control inspection, the items that need to be fixed are divided into two parts: "Section 1" and "Section 2". Your lender will require "Section 1" items to be fixed because they are the most critical. Most lenders will ignore "Section 2", except for VA and a few other lenders, which will require "Section 2" items to also be fixed.

A sample pest control report is included in appendix and also on our website. You can review it to see the difference between "Section 1" and "Section 2".

Usually, the seller is responsible to fix these items in his house. However, either the buyer or seller can fix these items, because it is negotiable. Most likely, you have already requested that the seller fix the pest control items when you wrote it into your Purchase Offer.

Your lender will not fund your loan until the work is completed and they receive an official Certification of Clearance from the pest control company. So you will want to make sure these repairs get done right away. If the home needs to be tented, that must be scheduled well in advance of the escrow closing date.

Your REALTOR®, home inspector, or pest control inspector may recommend that you get further inspections. For example, they may recommend a roof inspection or a foundation inspection. If the house has a water well or a septic tank, you will probably have to get those inspected, too.

Again, you can either pay for the inspections yourself or you can request that the seller pay for those items. Your REALTOR® will guide you through that process.

Want a FREE Home Warranty?

As we discussed earlier, everything is negotiable! One thing you always want is a home warranty. Why not get one FREE from the seller? After all, the sellers don't want you to have any problems with the house after you buy it. It is to their advantage to pay for your new home warranty! Ask the seller to pay for a 1 year home warranty policy. Your agent can request this warranty in your offer.

After it expires, you can pay the annual fee to renew it each year. You will find a home warranty very handy and, most importantly, it eliminates the stress that happens when things break around the house. I recommend renewing your home warranty every year. As the saying goes: *Hope for the best, but plan for the worst.*

It Gives You Peace of Mind

Rest assured that if anything breaks, you can get it fixed for only the cost of a service call fee. A home warranty will not prevent things from breaking. However, it will give you peace of mind that you won't have to pay thousands of dollars if something major breaks, such as the furnace or the water heater. Home warranty policies will not pay for lack of maintenance, such as a roof that was neglected. It often covers most appliances, plumbing, electric, and the heating system.

You simply pay a flat co-payment, usually about $50, and the home warranty company will pay the balance. It covers most things, so be sure to check your policy and see what is included. Certain items are excluded from the basic policy. For an additional fee, your home warranty can include things such as the air conditioner, spa, refrigerator, and roof. Again, you should negotiate this up front with the seller.

Mandatory Builder Warranties

You've already asked the seller to purchase a 1-year home warranty for you, and that is great. But if you're buying a brand new home, the builder may be required to provide you with specific types of new home construction warranties. The reason is because many states have "lemon laws" designed to protect home buyers from brand new home defects.

Each state has legal requirements for new home developers and builders to provide certain minimum home warranties. For example, California has a "new construction defect law" which is a 1-year implied warranty for general construction, as well as other warranties for specific construction issues. If anything breaks during that time, the builder will fix it or replace it for you, depending on the coverage of the warranty.

> *"SB 800 [in California] also known as the "FIX IT" law:*
>
> - *"Requires that builders provide home owners with a minimum one-year express warranty;*
>
> - *"Provides 1-, 2-, 4-, and 10-year statutes of limitations for construction defect actions, depending on the system and product involved, with most issues under the 10-year statute of limitations."*
>
> *(Perkins, 2002)*

In addition to the mandatory builder home warranties required by state, we recommend that you also order a standard home warranty. This will help supplement the builder's warranty, which may have limitations. Again, we emphasize that brand new homes are **NOT** always perfect, and we recommend both a home inspection and a home warranty.

7. Sign the Purchase Offer

With today's technology tools, you have the choice to sign your purchase offer in many different ways:

- Print out the offer and sign the papers with a pen

- Receive an email and sign it online using electronic signatures (such as DocuSign)
- Sign it on a tablet computer using a stylus or your finger

Sign the Purchase Offer

The last step is to apply your signature to your offer so it can be submitted to the seller's agent. Hopefully, your REALTOR® is set up with a mobile office and you can sign it online; but if not, you can sign the old fashioned way on printed paper. The offer package will probably include a few other documents, such as required disclosures.

Attach your EMD, Approval letter, and POF

Your Earnest Money Deposit (EMD) check is usually $1,000 or more, even if you have a "zero down" loan. You already wrote out your check earlier, and gave a copy to your REALTOR® remember?

Along with the purchase offer, your REALTOR® will need to submit this copy of your EMD check, lender approval letter, and POF (Proof of Funds), which verifies you have the funds available for down payment and closing costs.

Sign the Offer Digitally on the Computer

If your agent is set up to work paperlessly, he can send you the offer on email via DocuSign or other approved online signing service. Select your favorite signature, and then simply click the yellow arrow to sign your name. Better yet, if your REALTOR® has a tablet like an iPad, you can sign the offer with a stylus pen on the spot!

Be sure to get a copy of the offer sent to your email so you will have the file in your records. You don't have to print it out, if you want to have a paperless office just like your agent. Just make sure you have a copy for your files.

STEP 5: Purchase Contract

Can you believe it? We are already at Step 5, the purchase contract! Depending upon your state, your Realtor® will use a standard state Realtor®-approved form. Remember that every contract is going to be unique to your geographic area, your new house, and your situation.

California REALTORS® use a standard purchase offer, called an RPA-CA form. It also does triple duty as the purchase contract and the escrow opening instructions. It is from the California Association of REALTORS®, (C.A.R.) drawn up by top attorneys. Their forms are tried and true from usage throughout the years.

Now it is time for you to take a look at the following items:

- Major items in purchase contract
- Major closing costs for buyers
- Notes

We are going to review some of the major items that will be included in the sales contract. Also, we are going to discuss the major closing costs that buyers may have to pay. Then we have a few tips that you can note for future. Remember that each state, county, and region has its own unique contracts and customary procedures, but the process is similar.

1. Major Items in Purchase Contract

Let's now review the major items that will be in your purchase contract. We know this will vary from region to region; however, the basics will be similar no matter where you live.

The major terms in the sales contract include: amount of initial deposit; type and amount of mortgage financing; which parties will pay which closing costs; contingencies and conditions, and closing date. You are going to go over each of these items with your REALTOR® before signing and submitting your offer; but let's review each item now so you will feel prepared.

Sales Price

The first thing you will notice in your purchase contract is the sales price. That always seems to be the most important factor. Although you as the buyer offered a certain price, the seller may have made a counter offer for a different price. So the final sales price is what you both agree on when the negotiations are successful.

Remember that today, when you write your offer, this price is just the starting point, and it may not be the final sales price.

Property Address and APN (Tax Parcel Number)

The contract will show the complete property address, including street address, unit number (if any), city, state, and zip code. The contract will have the tax identification number from the county property tax records, which we in California refer to as the APN (assessor's parcel number) — a code that is assigned by the county tax assessor office. It helps to identify the legal description of a property.

The legal description is a narrative description, which can be several sentences or several paragraphs long. It is listed on the deeds when they are recorded, but usually not listed on the purchase contract. On the purchase contract, it's summarized by using the address and tax identification number.

Amount of Initial Deposit

The purchase contract shows how much money you are putting down as part of your initial deposit, called the earnest money deposit. This is the first part of your down payment, and you will pay the rest of your down payment shortly before the closing date.

For example, you write a check for $1,000 as your earnest money deposit, but your total down payment is $5,000, so that means you'll have to pay the additional $4,000 down payment shortly before closing.

Terms of Mortgage Financing

What type of loan are you approved for? An FHA or a VA loan? A conventional loan? How much total money are you putting down, and how much are you borrowing from your mortgage lender? Will you have 1 loan or 2 loans? Are you asking the seller to carry back part of the purchase price as seller financing? Will you be receiving down payment assistance from a nonprofit agency? These items should all be covered in the purchase contract.

If you have a specific type of loan, such as VA, FHA, or USDA, you should disclose your loan type because those government loans have special circumstances. Specific loans such as VA will affect the seller and the transaction so the seller will need to know right up front.

Which Party Pays what Closing Costs

Your contract will specify which party will pay which closing costs. Each region typically splits the fees according to that region's customs; but again, this is a point of negotiation between the buyer and the seller. Often a first-time homebuyer will ask the seller to pay part of the closing costs, or may receive financial assistance to help with the costs. If so, this would be part of the financial package.

Contingencies and Conditions

What types of contingencies exist? A contingency is something that hinges on a certain condition happening, and in some regions is known as a "subject to". For example, California Association of Realtor's® standard RPA-CA purchase contract contains a 17-day contingency period. It means that the buyers have a right to inspect the property, investigate it, review reports, and do their research within the first 17 days. If the property does not meet their requirements within this 17-day contingency period, they can cancel the contract without losing their earnest money deposit.

Your REALTOR® will probably make sure the purchase contract is "subject to" an appraisal with the valuation at (or above) the agreed-upon purchase price. For example, if the purchase price is $200,000, but the appraisal values the house at only $180,000, then the buyer may cancel the purchase contract without penalty.

Fixtures Remaining in Home

Make a list of the appliances, fixtures, and personal property that you want to stay with the home, such as the stove, oven, dishwasher, refrigerator, and micro-hood. Other common items that are negotiable include the clothes washer and dryer, a specific chandelier, certain window coverings, workbenches, sheds, built-in stereo systems, or any other items. In real estate lingo, we say that these items "convey" with the purchase.

Be sure to list everything in your offer so there won't be any miscommunication later on. Remember that everyone has different expectations. You don't want to be disappointed when you counted on the fridge being there, but when you move in, it's gone.

Home Warranty

We also discussed the value and importance of a home warranty, and you can ask the seller to pay for it! A home warranty is similar to an insurance policy. It gives you peace of mind to know that if something breaks, you will not have to pay hundreds or thousands of dollars to fix it. So always ask for a home warranty with your purchase. In fact, ask the seller to pay for the home warranty so you can get it free.

Inspections

We now know how important it is to get a home inspection and review the report. The inspection will probably reveal some things that are wrong with the house and need to be fixed, or perhaps things which just need to be brought to your attention. Make sure you protect your interests by requesting a structural building inspection, also known as a home inspection. There will be additional inspections, such as a pest control inspection to check for termites and water damage.

Seller-Required Repairs, if any

If repairs need to be made, who is going to fix those items? The problem is that you usually would not have the results of the inspections until **AFTER** you write your offer, so you will not know what needs to be fixed until later.

In an ideal situation, the seller will have completed a home inspection before you wrote your offer; and if so, that's great. Read it thoroughly. In your offer, request the things you want fixed, and submit these items to be repaired on your offer. In this case, since you have a copy of the inspection before writing your offer, you would not be able to negotiate repairs later on.

In a pest control inspection, it is a little easier to negotiate repairs up front before the inspection is completed, because your lender will require "Section 1" work to be completed, and possibly "Section 2". Your offer already specifies who will pay for the report and each phase of the work to be done.

Real Estate Agent Representation

Which real estate agent and brokerage is representing the seller? This agent is known as the "listing agent" or the seller's agent. Who is representing the buyer? Your REALTOR® is the buyer's agent, and is also known as the "selling agent".

The parties, their agents, and the brokerage firms are listed on the contract. If the same brokerage is representing both the seller and the buyer, this is known as "dual agency". Your agent can give you disclosures that explain the difference.

Closing Date

You are going to request your preferred closing date. 30 days is considered a typical closing time, but if you have a challenging loan, it could be 45 to 60 days. If you are purchasing a bank-owned property, known as an REO, plan for at least a 60-day process. If you buy a short sale property, everyone is at the mercy of the bank, which is often a 3 to 6-month approval process, and it could be longer.

Our point is this: although you as the buyer will request a certain closing date, the actual date may be later than you expect. In addition, the seller may want to close escrow on a different date than you do, so that is another negotiating point. Remain flexible and realize that the dates may change as you go through the escrow process. Everyone needs to have a target closing date that they are aiming for, and the timeframe will become clearer as you proceed with your transaction.

Details of Escrow Transaction

Which escrow/settlement company or attorney service will be used to hold the deposit and conduct the closing? The title insurance vendor will also need to be selected. The title insurance policy is important because the title company will vouch for the sellers and insure the buyer's right of ownership. You will select other services and vendors also, and remember it is all negotiable upon mutual agreement of both parties — the buyer and the seller.

2. Major Closing Costs for Buyers

Now let's review and summarize the major closing costs that you as the buyer may be expected to pay or that you will encounter. It will be different for you depending on your region, your mortgage loan, and what you have negotiated on the purchase contract with the seller to be precise as to the closing costs.

If you have negotiated with the seller for him to pay part of your closing costs, it will typically be shown as a credit from him to you. Major closing costs that a Buyer may have to pay will include appraisal and inspection fees, mortgage loan fees, insurance premium, notary public signing fee, escrow reserves (refundable pad), and HOA fees, taxes, and interest (pro-rated).

These costs will be itemized on your HUD-1 settlement sheet, which lists all the fees due. We have included a sample HUD-1 as well as a sample closing statement from the escrow company, which you can see is much simpler to understand.

As soon as you open escrow, be sure to ask your escrow officer for a copy of the estimated HUD-1 so you can review it with your Realtor® for accuracy. Some costs will be pro-rated, in other words calculated based on a daily rate.

On the HUD-1, you will see the words "POC" which indicate that a fee was Paid Outside of Closing. That means it was already been paid and will not be calculated into your final closing costs. With that in mind, let's go through our list of closing costs.

Credit Report Fees

Your mortgage lender probably required you to pay for your credit report up front. If so, credit report fees will not be listed on your closing statement, or may be listed as POC (paid outside of closing).

Appraisal Fee

The appraisal fee varies but it will probably cost between $350 and $500. Most lenders will require you to pay this fee up front BEFORE they order the appraisal. They typically accept a credit card payment or a personal check written to the appraisal management company. So again, if you have paid for the appraisal up front, it will probably be listed on the closing statement as POC.

Paying the appraisal is a slight risk, because if you cancel the purchase of this home, the appraisal would have been a waste of your money. So make sure that you are committed to this home purchase before you order the appraisal. Remember, the appraisal must be completed within the timeframe required by your purchase contract.

Building Inspection Fees

In many areas, the home building inspection is the responsibility of the buyer, whereas the seller pays the pest control inspection. The buyer usually pays any additional inspections, unless you requested that the seller pay it. Most likely, these items will be paid at the time of the inspection; but in some cases, they are billed to escrow and then you will see them on the closing statement.

Insurance Premium

Another closing cost would be annual insurance premiums. You will need fire insurance coverage on your house, also known as hazard insurance or homeowners insurance. It will be required by your mortgage lender. You will usually pay a one year policy in advance, and will pay it out of escrow. So you will see it itemized on the HUD-1.

> *"Homeowner's insurance protects you against substantial financial loss resulting from damage to your home, injury to a visitor while on your property, damage to the contents of your home, and loss of personal property due to theft or vandalism." p.8 (Rowley, 2007)*

Interest on Mortgage Loan (pro-rated)

You will have to pay interest on your new mortgage loan, and it will be pro-rated depending upon what day it closes and when your next payment is due. Your mortgage lender can explain that to you in more detail. The monthly mortgage loan payment includes both principal and interest; the principal is paid in advance and the interest is paid in arrears. Depending on the date of the loan funding and the date of closing, you will pay pro-rated interest on your closing statement.

County Property Taxes (pro-rated)

Your county property taxes will also be pro-rated, again depending upon the closing date and the date that your next payment is due. Most counties require that the annual property tax be paid twice per year, so the escrow company will calculate exactly how much is owed.

HOA Fees (pro-rated)

If there are HOA or other fees due, they will be pro-rated as of the tentative closing date and listed on the closing statement. Pro-rated means that it will calculate on a daily rate and charge to each party accordingly. For example, with a month that has 30 days, if escrow closes on the 15th of the month, then the seller will pay half of that month's HOA and you, the buyer, will pay the other half.

Along with monthly HOA fees, most HOA management companies will also charge transfer fees and document preparation fees, which can be quite hefty. Usually the seller is responsible to pay these fees — but, again, it is subject to negotiation. What did you write in your offer? What did you and the seller mutually agree to? Look at your purchase offer.

Loan Underwriting, Mortgage Fees, and Lender's Title Insurance

Unless you are paying all cash for your purchase, there will be various loan fees associated with your mortgage loan. You will see them itemized on your Good Faith Estimate form, as well as on page 2 of your HUD-1 closing statement. Some of the fees may be negotiable, but most loan mortgage fees will not be waived.

Escrow Reserves (refundable pad)

The escrow/settlement company may collect escrow reserve funds, which is a refundable "pad" of extra money, just in case your costs are more than expected. That could easily happen if escrow closes on a different day than you planned, because some costs are pro-rated per day. Upon close of escrow, you will receive a check in the mail for any funds you have overpaid.

Notary or Legal Services

When you sign the loan paperwork, you will need to have some documents notarized by a Notary Public. The Notary usually charges a document signing fee, which may be paid by your mortgage lender and then you will be expected to reimburse the fee through escrow payment.

Escrow, Title, and Attorney Services

You will have to pay either escrow/settlement fees or attorney closing fees, depending upon your state. In California, we pay escrow fees, which are usually split between buyer and seller. Also, there will be 2 types of title insurance: the seller's title insurance, which is typically paid by the seller, and title insurance for your new loan, which would be your responsibility.

> *"Title insurance in the United States is insurance which ensures that you have clear and marketable title to a property when you purchase it. Title insurance has many facets to it like lien searches, title commitments, title policies etc." (Levinrad, 2009)*

Recording Services and Title-Related Services

The escrow company will probably also charge you some additional fees, such as courier fees, overnight delivery, and document preparation. Some of these fees may be negotiable with the escrow company. If you are unsure, ask your escrow officer to explain the fees.

Conclusion

Now you can see why we advised you to save up some money and be prepared for these expenses. If the cost seems extreme, don't get worried. Many of the fees are included in your loan, or will be paid by the seller as negotiated in your purchase contract. As a bonus, perhaps you have found a source of down payment assistance in your area that can help pay money towards your closing costs.

On the HUD-1, you can see your bottom line on Line 303. Look at page 1, the bottom left, and you will see the amount the buyer (you) will have to pay in cash, or the amount that will be refunded back to the buyer. If there is an "X" in front of the word "FROM", the buyer will have to pay this amount. If there is an "X" in front of the word "TO", the buyer will receive a refund of this amount.

3. Notes

The buyer typically does not have to pay their REALTOR®'s compensation because the commission for both agents is paid by the seller.

Real Estate Commissions are Typically Paid by the Seller

In most states, including California, the real estate commissions are paid by the seller. That's right — the compensation for the seller's agent AND the buyer's agent are already covered for you! The seller will receive a separate HUD-1 showing his own expenses, and the total real estate commission is included. Therefore, you will not see your buyer's agent compensation on your HUD-1 settlement statement.

Transaction Fees and Closing Costs

Costs are customarily split between buyers and sellers differently in each area. This list of closing costs and fees varies by region and depends upon the county and state in which that the home is located. Some areas have costs that others do not. Again, this just emphasizes the importance of hiring a local REALTOR® to guide you through the process!

Do Not Feel Overwhelmed

Remember that your REALTOR® is experienced in this process. Your real estate agent has helped many first time homebuyers, just like you, and he or she will walk you through every step. Hire the right professionals and keep a positive attitude. Help is on the way!

STEP 6: Negotiations

What is negotiation? That is when the buyer and seller are discussing what each party will give and take. Each party will win certain points when they agree to allow the other party to win some points also. It is communicating back and forth until all parties come to a mutual agreement.

> **"Negotiation is a field of knowledge and endeavor that focuses on gaining the favor of people from whom we want things. It's as simple as that."**
> **p.15 (Cohen, 1982)**

Negotiation of price and terms on the purchase contract are aspects of the sale.

1. Negotiations
2. Counter offer
3. Negotiating process
4. Continue shopping
5. Further negotiations
6. Document review
7. Pack for your move
8. Keep a backup plan

Now we are at the phase called "negotiations". This is where the buyer and the seller finalize the purchase price, agree on all the terms of the offer, and prepare the transaction for closing. If there is any part of the home buying process that causes anxiety, it is often the negotiating step.

Nothing is certain yet. You don't know if the seller is going to accept your offer or will counter offer back. You don't know what the final price is or what your moving date will be. You do not yet know what the inspection will say about the home's condition, or what the seller will agree to fix. Then, there is the question of how much money you are going to have to pay for closing costs.

Yes, at this point, there are unknown factors. Have faith and know that everything will be resolved soon. It is simply a matter of going through the process. Just put your best foot forward and continue to make progress every day. Continue working toward your goal and your dream of home ownership.

My best advice is: **Don't become emotionally attached to the home yet. Remember, at this point it is still a business transaction.**

In this step, we are going to talk about negotiation and your counter offer. The negotiation phase involves going back and forth between the buyer and the seller until you have come to a mutual agreement on the price and terms. Then, we will discuss the negotiating process itself and the next steps.

You should continue shopping for homes as part of your backup plan — not making offers on them, but simply being aware of homes that are available and keeping your options open. It is important to know what else is available on the market so you can continue making good financial decisions, rather than being attached to 1 home.

Further negotiations may develop along the way, after you have an inspection performed. We are going to talk about reviewing documents with your REALTOR®, who is your trusted advisor to guide you through the process.

1. Negotiations

This begins the negotiation phase. Don't worry, your trusty real estate agent will be there to negotiate on your behalf, and get you the best price and terms. Your agent will guide you as to the best way to respond to the seller.

Some people may shy away from negotiating, but remember, it's a critical part of everyday life. Just as you get your children to eat their vegetables, and just like you know how to ask your boss for a raise, you can use those same skills to get the best deal for your family.

> *"Negotiation is the heart of human interaction. Every time people interact, there is negotiation going on: verbally or nonverbally, consciously or unconsciously...That doesn't mean you have to actively negotiate everything in your life all the time. But it does mean that those who are more conscious of the interactions around them get more of what they want in life." p.3 (Diamond, 2010)*

Once the seller receives your purchase offer, they can choose to:

- Accept your offer exactly as it is written
- Reject your offer by letting your agent know he will not accept it
- Send you a counter offer
- Ignore your offer and not respond back

Sellers Can Accept, Reject, or Ignore your Purchase Offer

When you submit your offer to the seller, you are very excited and hope that the seller will accept your offer. However, the seller may not accept your offer, unless it is a very strong offer or the seller is highly motivated. Be ready for a counter offer and some further negotiations.

One of our secret tips is writing a personal letter with your heart-warming story. To assist with negotiations, consider writing a letter from you and your family. Your REALTOR® would submit this letter with your offer. Some of our tips are:

- Explain to the seller that you are first-time homebuyers and you are excited about buying his house
- Let him or her know that you will take good care of the house, and how much your family will love the home
- Give specific examples of how the home will benefit you
- Show an attitude of gratitude and perhaps it will touch the seller's heart

Often this was the first home for the seller's family too, and hopefully, they can relate to your story. If so, he will want to bless you and your family just like he and his family were blessed to own the home. A personal letter can move the seller so much, that he will want to sell his house to you rather than to a cash investor who submits a higher offer.

I find that owner-occupant buyers (families who will live in the home they buy) are often outbid by cash investors. If you can appeal to the seller's emotions (based on price, personal needs, or positive comments) you may get the seller to say "yes" to your offer instead of higher-priced bids! Sometimes, I help my buyers write a nice letter to the sellers.

***For example**: "Dear Mr. and Mrs. Seller, we love your beautiful home. We are first-time homebuyers and excited to purchase our very first house! Our son Jimmy has been begging us for a dog for the past two years, but our landlord does not allow dogs. When we viewed your home, Jimmy got excited and wanted to move in right away so he could finally get his puppy and play catch in the back yard. We really, really want to buy your home and we hope you can strongly consider our competitive offer. We promise to maintain this lovely home in great condition through the years as our family grows up here. We appreciate your consideration and Jimmy says 'thank you' too!"*

The Seller Can Make You a Counter Offer

The counter offer is usually a higher price than you offered or a change of terms. Once you get the counter offer back from the seller, you can accept it, reject it, or counter offer again. This is all part of the negotiation process.

Your REALTOR® will advise you of the pros and cons of the counter offer, just like he explained the offer to you initially. He will show you your options and help you discuss the consequences of each option, but, ultimately, the choice is yours.

2. Counter Offer

The counter offer process continues between seller and buyer until one of the following situations develops:

- The seller and buyer agree on a mutually acceptable price and terms
- Either the seller or the buyer decides to stop negotiating, thereby cancelling the offer

Multiple Counter Offers

After the offer, the buyer and seller may go back and forth with multiple counter offers to arrive at a mutually acceptable final sale price and terms.

In the counter offer stage, the buyer and seller will go back and forth with counter offers. It is a give-and-take process and neither party will get all of their wishes. Eventually, both seller and buyer will come to an agreement on the price and terms, which means that both parties have to give a little bit. The counter offer phase may continue for a few days or maybe even a couple of weeks. Your goal is to come to an agreement on the price and terms with the seller.

End of Negotiations

If you keep going back and forth and are not able to come to an agreement, then the negotiations will end without an executed contract. One of the parties will drop out of the negotiating process and move on to other buyers or sellers.

For example, the seller receives other buyer offers and decides to accept one of them or perhaps you and your family determine that the seller is not going to agree to a price that fits your budget, so you cancel your offer and move on to view other homes.

3. Negotiating Process

Why does your REALTOR® advise you to offer a fair price? Why does she request a quick turnaround time for the offer acceptance?

- Until the sellers accept your offer, they can continue to review and accept other offers.
- The quicker you get your offer approved, the less chance that another buyer will get the property.

During this negotiating process, until all parties finalize the contract, the seller can and will continue to accept other offers. Now you are in the negotiating process. While the buyer and seller are negotiating, the contract is still open. In other words, the contract is not completely final. The purchase offer is in limbo. Until both the buyer and seller finalize and agree upon the contract in writing, the seller can continue to accept other offers, and probably will continue to receive offers from buyers. During the negotiation process, if the seller receives a better offer from another buyer, she may decide to take that offer.

Sellers Continue to Accept Offers

If the seller gets an offer better than yours, he may take the other offer instead. It is important to offer your highest price and best terms in your initial purchase offer. When you offer your best price up front, and you do not request too many concessions, the seller will be inclined to accept your offer right away without a counter offer. This puts you in the best position of securing your purchase immediately, and then the seller cannot back out, change his mind, or accept another offer.

That is why it is important to offer a fair price and request quick turnaround times for contract acceptance. Your agent will request a quick turnaround time for the seller to respond to your offer. Although the standard time for a response in California is 3 days for an offer, I often request a turnaround time of only 1 day on my buyers' offers. This strategy does not give the seller much time to receive and review offers from other buyers, which is exactly our plan!

4. Continue Shopping

Once you have submitted your purchase offer, be prepared to continue shopping for houses. Do not become emotionally attached to the house yet because you will need a backup plan, just in case.

If Both Parties Do Not Agree, Continue Shopping and Find Another Home

Now we are going to talk about shopping for your house. After you have made an offer on your favorite house, keep in mind that the seller may not agree, or she may come back with a counter offer that is higher than what you want to pay. Therefore, you should continue looking at houses for sale as a backup plan. It is always good to have a plan B, and even plans C, D, and E.

Your REALTOR® will advise you whether you should make offers on other houses while you have a counter offer outstanding. In most cases, my buyers only have 1 offer outstanding at a time. After you have submitted an offer, you typically do not want to make offers on other houses. That could complicate matters.

For example, if you submit offers to 2 different sellers and both of them decide to accept your offer, then you will have to cancel 1 of the offers, or you may even be legally obligated to continue both contracts.

Get Excited, but Not Emotionally Hooked on the Home (Yet)

Yes, you will be very excited about buying your first home and relieved to have made your first offer, but realize that most offers are not accepted when they are submitted. Often the seller will counter offer or accept an offer from another buyer. This is real life — it is not like the TV show where buyers always get their first offer accepted and have a happy ending in 30 minutes. So don't become too excited just yet, or you may be let down when you don't get the house.

If you become too excited, your emotions can interfere with making good financial and business decisions. What if the seller comes back with an offer higher than your budget allows? You should use good business sense and counter offer at a price that you can afford, or back out of the transaction and look for different house. However, if you are emotionally attached, you might be tempted to give in and pay the price that is above your budget. That would not be a good financial decision for your family.

5. Further Negotiations

After the initial price and terms are agreed upon, there are often re-negotiations between the buyer and seller. The main cause of re-negotiations is due to repair items found in a home inspection report.

As a buyer, it is your responsibility to do your "due diligence" by investigating the condition of the house. For example, you may see a room that looks sub-standard. If so, you should check with the county building department to verify if the room was built with a permit or not. If not, as the new owner, you may later be required to tear it down at your expense. Worse, it could have faulty wiring or plumbing because it wasn't built to conform with building codes.

> *"When certain additions or revisions have been made to a home, approved permits should be on file with the local building department. Approved permits will help assure you that the building department has inspected and accepted the construction work as that of being safe and proper." p.8 (Charloff, 2011)*

In many areas of the United States, homes are built with attics and basements. If they were converted into bedrooms, research them to see if they are permitted as living areas before you close escrow. In areas where homes are smaller, such as California, it is very common that home owners convert their garage to additional living space. So when you find that "perfect" den conversion in the garage, you should be aware that it may not have building permits.

> *"Zoning regulations might require the existence of a garage or a carport on a residential property. It is not uncommon to find that a garage has been later converted to another use and no new garage or carport has since been built to suit the locality's covered car parking requirement. As such, this conversion would be in violation of local zoning regulations." p.42 (Charloff, 2011)*

Final Sales Price may be Negotiated even Further

Depending upon the results of the home inspection and other reports, you may want to modify the price and terms. Maybe you had a home inspection, and discovered some items that need to be fixed.

So your REALTOR® sends the seller a Repair Request asking for those items to be fixed. This is another point of negotiation. Just when you thought you were done, the seller comes back with a revision to the repair request. It means you need to negotiate again.

Until all parties agree on all terms of the purchase, there still is room for negotiation. So, be prepared to go back to the drawing board, to revisit the negotiating table, and continue hashing things out if necessary.

The Problem with Post-Offer Home Inspections

The challenge is that most sellers do not perform home inspections when they first list their house for sale. Therefore, the inspection is not completed until **AFTER** you and the seller have agreed on the final price and terms. After that, you receive the results of the home inspection, and notice things that you want fixed. Then you will request that the seller fix certain items at his expense.

As we discussed earlier, that's why it is so important to perform the home inspection as soon as possible, before your contingency period has elapsed, and before you sign off on the final contract by satisfying (or removing) your contingencies.

6. Document Review?

It is optional to have your attorney review the contract that is a standard form from a REALTOR® Association.

REALTOR® Standard Contract Forms

These standard Realtor® forms were written with input from top real estate attorneys and are fair to all parties. When you see unfamiliar documents, such as contracts from the stationery store, you may start thinking about having your attorney review the documents.

Keep in mind that most REALTORS® use standard forms from their Association of REALTOR®'S office. Attorneys in each state who are familiar with real estate laws write the standard contracts and supporting forms. The forms are written to help make the transaction fair to both the buyers and the sellers. These forms are revised periodically to reflect new laws and changes in the real estate industry so they are kept up-to-date.

In fact, in California, our attorneys at the California Association of REALTORS® (C.A.R.) examine recent lawsuits and incorporate better terms into each form so that we can all avoid lawsuits!

Forms are Time-Tested and Approved by Many Attorneys

If you feel more comfortable having your attorney review your documents that is just fine. As a consumer, you have every right to get your contracts reviewed by your legal counsel. Some buyers have an attorney on retainer and they simply fax the purchase contract and loan summary to their attorney. Buyers who are LegalShield© members may want to use the contract-review service included as part of their membership benefits.

Remember that when another person reviews your documents, it will add time to the purchase process. So be sure to plan ahead and have your attorney review the documents early on. If you want to have your attorney review your documents, send them to the attorney's office as soon as you get the copies.

Plan Ahead if You Want your Attorney to Review the Documents

Most buyers do not have an attorney review their documents. They realize these are standard forms prepared by their trusted REALTOR® and, therefore, they feel comfortable with the documents.

However, if you insist on having your attorney review everything, please inform your REALTOR® ahead of time so it will not delay the closing. If your attorney recommends any changes, they will need to be incorporated into the negotiation process before all the terms and documents are finalized. That is another reason to get your legal advice as early as possible.

7. Pack for Your Move

You have finished your negotiations, signed the final purchase contract and released the contingencies. Now you need to start packing boxes for your move.

Start Packing your House!

Okay, are you ready to pack for your move? It is time to start thinking about how you are going to be transitioning into your new house. Even though you do not have your house for sure yet, it is time to start planning the moving process. Most likely, you will be closing escrow on your house within the next 2 to 3 weeks.

You can find helpful packing tips at ***www.MeatheadMovers.com***. One great tip is to start gathering as many boxes as possible. Also, gather packing supplies, such as bubble wrap and foam "peanuts".

What do you pack? First, pack the items that you do not use very often. Lastly, pack the items you use every day and will need when you first move in. Label items using sticky notes. Label boxes using a black permanent marker. Box up each room and label each box: kitchen, bedroom, bathroom, etc. Packing and moving take much longer than you think — so it is best to start early. It will help your move be easy, enjoyable and stress-free.

Get rid of things you don't need anymore. If you are like me, and like most Americans, you have a lot of furniture and stuff. If you do not want to move clutter to your new house, now is a good time to get rid of it. Here's an easy rule of thumb: Dispose of anything you have not used in the last 6 months. I know it is hard to part with our "things", but remember you can give your furniture, clothing, and household goods to charity.

Begin cleaning out your garage, backyard, attic, and basement. Give away as many things as you can. I would guesstimate that up to 50% of your household goods are not being used. When you give away these items to needy families and charities, you are helping others.

You are recycling too, which is great for our environment. By making a tax-deductible donation to Goodwill, Salvation Army, or your local thrift store, you'll be doing a good deed while you pare down your clutter. Imagine moving into your new home with a fresh, clean start.

Now we need to think about how you are going to move your things. How far is the move? Across town or across country? Will you hire a moving company or will you employ the "family and friends" moving method? If you are paying a moving company, they will do a lot of the packing and moving for you, BUT you still have to label everything so you will know what is in each box after you move.

Transfer Utilities and Change your Mailing Address

Next, you should start the process of transferring your utilities and changing your address for your mail.

Notify your Landlord of your Move-Out

Also, you should review your lease to see how much advance notice you need to give to your landlord before you move out. Give your formal written "notice to move" to your landlord about 2 weeks before your closing date. Some leases require 30 or 60 days' notice to move out.

Be sure to give the adequate notice to your landlord to stay in compliance with your lease. You want to have overlapping time between your old house and your new house, just in case escrow does not close on time. It is helpful to have plenty of time to move and then you would not be frazzled.

Packing and Moving Requires Effort and Can be Stressful for Everyone

Even though you and your family are thrilled to be moving into your very own home, the process of buying a house, packing, and moving can be very stressful. Moving is a major life experience. You may find yourselves snapping at each other because of the tension. Remind your family members that you are all working toward a common goal and building your dream together.

Remember, there will be emotions, including joy and tears, during your home buying process. You can expect ups and downs, twists and turns, and unexpected excitement. There may be some intense negotiations, frustrations and disappointments. You will also experience high points, such as the excitement of finding your dream home, writing an offer, getting your offer accepted, closing escrow, and moving in with your new keys in your hand!

Stay Excited Enough to Give You Energy to Pack

So you are going to have to manage your emotions. If you find yourself feeling overwhelmed, anxious, nervous, or worried, take a break from the home buying process.

Take a short breather with the family and take a day trip somewhere nearby. Let your REALTOR® know that you may be away from your computer, but you will still be available by cell phone. Pause — take a moment to reflect on how grateful you are to have the opportunity for your dream home. You will feel much better once you put your life into perspective. You will come back excited again and ready to complete the home buying process.

8. Keep a Backup Plan

What are the reasons NOT to get your hopes up too high in the beginning of the escrow?

- Many transactions "fall out" of escrow and you may be disappointed

- So you can make a good business decision to cancel your contract if needed
- Keep a backup plan for the other houses you liked

Many Transactions "Fall Out" of Escrow

Okay, you are now in escrow. You hope to be closing on your new house in about 2 weeks so you are packing and preparing, and starting to get excited. However, you don't want to get your hopes up too high. At this point, many transactions still cancel for various reasons. Don't be too disappointed if, for some reason, you don't get this house.

Be Prepared to Back Out if Needed

Do not become so emotionally attached to this house that you cannot make a good business decision to back out if you find out that it has major problems.

If the house has major problems revealed by a home inspection, you may have to make the decision to cancel the purchase and back out. So, try not to get emotionally attached to this particular house.

Keep a Backup Plan for Other Houses You Liked

At this point, you probably stopped looking at other houses for sale. However, you still need to make a note of other houses you liked, just in case. Remember what we advised about having plans B, C, and D.

Throughout my many years of experience helping first-time homebuyers, I have seen plans change at a moment's notice. That is why it is always best to be prepared. You have heard the saying: *Plan for the worst, but hope for the best*. That is great advice to heed.

STEP 7: Escrow Process

Let's discuss the escrow process and the steps involved. Escrow steps typically happen in this order.

1. Open escrow
2. Home inspection and reports
3. Order appraisal
4. Sign disclosures
5. Review title report
6. Get home insurance
7. Final loan approval
8. Plan your moving date

First, we are going to discuss how escrow opens and the documents that are needed to start an escrow. Some important things we're going to do during the escrow process are: order a home inspection and other reports, read and review those reports, order an appraisal and review it, sign disclosures, order a title report and review it, get home insurance, and cooperate with our lender to get final loan approval.

Your REALTOR® will guide you through the process by ordering reports and explaining the documents. If you do not understand everything right now, don't worry. Your REALTOR® will be with you every step of the way. Finally, it is now time to plan our moving date. So let's get started with Step 7 now!

1. Open Escrow

Congratulations! Now that your offer is accepted, you are officially "under contract". Typically, you will give the escrow company (or settlement company) your earnest money deposit (EMD). It means you are considered "in escrow" or "under contract".

> *"Escrow is a means for enabling ownership transfers to occur fairly and squarely… an impartial third party… sees that the buyer and seller perform as they have agreed… Escrow enables a buyer and seller to do business with minimum risk, because the responsibility for handling the funds and documents is placed in the hands of someone who is not… affected by the outcome. The escrow holder is a disinterested go-between for the parties involved in the transaction, one whose legal obligation is to safeguard the interests of everyone who is affected by the outcome." p.1 (Gadow, 2003)*

In some cases, such as a short sale, you may not open escrow right away. Instead, you may have to wait until after seller's short sale lender has approved the transaction. In a short sale, the opening of escrow may be delayed, as well as the timeline for inspections, reports, and disclosures.

Take your EMD Check to the Escrow Office

Okay, now you are ready to open escrow. After your purchase offer is accepted and the seller signs the contract to accept your offer, your REALTOR® will take the documents to the escrow company and you will take your earnest money deposit check to the escrow officer. In some states, this may be an attorney or a settlement officer.

I recommend taking a money order or a cashier check, rather than a personal check. Certified funds would be a money order or a cashier's check. We recommend certified funds because if your check bounces, you may jeopardize your escrow and lose your house. Escrow companies generally will not accept cash. It is important to meet the escrow/settlement officer in person and develop a good working relationship. After all, this officer will be working for YOU. Or, you can simply send the funds via wire transfer from your bank. If you do, be sure to verify with your agent first. And go meet the escrow officer anyway… that personal relationship is critical!

> *"In many states, especially in the East, attorneys handle the closing. The attorney may order the title search and issue the title insurance policy. Your attorney will be responsible for reviewing the documents and coordinating the closing with your lender." p.6 (Gadow, 2003)*

The escrow officer is a neutral party who ensures that "concurrent performance" takes place. In other words, the deed that transfers title on the property from seller to buyer will be recorded at the county courthouse, and at the same time the buyer's funds are released to the seller and other parties to be paid. The escrow officer orders the deed to be recorded only after all obligations (such as mortgage loans, title insurance cost, inspection fees, and termite clearance bills) are paid. The escrow company guarantees that your money is taken care of properly and legally and that your real estate transaction will occur with concurrent performance.

A Title Officer Examines the Property's Chain of Title

The escrow officer will now order a title report from a title company. The title officer will review the public records relating to your property to determine if there is an insurable chain of title.

> *"Depending on where you live, your title company may be an attorney, an independent title company, or a large national title company. Whoever performs the title search and issues the policy of title insurance will be responsible for searching the title and determining if the seller has legal right to convey title to the new buyer. The title company will list all the items relevant to your parcel of land and report them to you."*
> *p.5 (Gadow, 2003)*

You will receive a copy of the preliminary title report, also referred to as a "prelim", which you should review with your real estate agent. You will receive a final title report later on.

Escrow is Sometimes Delayed

In California, a standard escrow period is 30 to 45 days — or at least it used to be. With distressed properties, escrows often take longer because they are delayed. For example, if you are buying a short sale home, the process may take 3 to 6 months. REO (bank owned properties) take longer to close. Also, if you are receiving a government loan such as VA, FHA, or USDA, escrow will probably be 45 or 60 days instead of the standard 30 days.

In addition to the escrow period to which both parties have agreed, be aware that there may be delays. Some of the reasons that cause a delayed transaction include: your mortgage loan process takes longer than normal to process your loan, or repairs take longer than anticipated.

2. Home Inspection and Reports

A physical structural inspection is a critical part of your home purchase. Here is what you need to know about ordering a home inspection:

- Your REALTOR® will help you order a home inspection and schedule it
- There may be other reports you need also
- The reports must be completed within the inspection timeframe required by your offer
- Review the results of these inspections with your REALTOR®
- If you want the seller to repair anything, you must ask for it in writing before your contingency period expires

Order a Home Inspection and Other Reports

Now let's talk about home inspections and reports. This is a very important part of the home buying process. You will need to order a home inspection and other reports. Based on the results of the home inspection, the report may recommend that you conduct other inspections, such as a roof inspection, the foundation inspection, a plumbing inspection, or electrical inspection. Here in California, we also request a pest control report to determine if there is termite damage in the home.

You can select any licensed vendor of your choosing. However, it is a good idea to ask your REALTOR® for names of home inspectors who have conducted good inspections with other buyers. She should be able to give you a list of 3 good home inspectors so you can select 1 that you like. Hire a great home inspector, someone you can trust, who has an excellent reputation in the community.

As the homebuyer, you should meet the home inspector at your new house for the home inspection. I recommend that you meet him near the END of his inspection. If you arrive when he first starts his work, he will be annoyed with you watching him for three hours.

However, if you arrive during the last 30 minutes of the inspection, he will gladly summarize all items he found on his report. He should also take you and show you the "trouble spots" in the house. Although the report will not be completed yet, a good home inspector will take time to explain his findings and answer your questions.

Additional Inspections, Reports, and Requests

Be aware that a rural property will not have standard public utilities, but instead it may have a septic tank, a water well, solar panels, wind turbines, a satellite dish, and a propane tank for fuel. Be prepared to ask for (and pay for) an inspection of each item.

If it's a brand new house, or a newer building, ask the seller for blueprints, floor plans, building specifications, architectural, structural, and mechanical plans. Older houses probably won't have that available, but when there have been add-ons, you should ask for remodeling plans and copies of permits.

Get appliances warranties and manuals from the seller. If the seller has painted the house, ask the seller to leave cans of paint in the garage, so you can color match later on.

Don't Skip the Inspections!

If you're crunched for time, you may be tempted to take a short cut and NOT order an inspection. Always order an inspection by a quality home inspector, even if your prospective home is brand new! Why? Because all homes have issues, and no house is built perfectly. Mike Holmes in his book, "The Holmes Inspection" reveals why brand new houses may have defects.

> *"Builders have a lot of people working for them, so many that it's hard to really achieve quality control. There are always a lot of subcontractors on big builds in new housing developments, and lots of workers who don't last long on the job - so can the builders really guarantee the skill and integrity of every person who works on every house? No, they can't... When people rush, they get sloppy." (Holmes, 2012) page 201.*

And be sure to check the credentials, experience, and knowledge of your inspector. If try to save money by asking your uncle to take a look at the house, he may not be trained in all the aspects needed for a complete inspection, even if he's a licensed contractor.

The bottom line is: always get an inspection and review it. Ask questions, and get further inspections if needed. Your research is called the buyer's "due diligence." It's YOUR job to protect you and your family.

Review the Results with your REALTOR®

Since you went to the home inspection and met the home inspector, you already know what to expect on the report. If you could not attend the home inspection, your REALTOR® can give you a summary of what the inspector found. Most home inspection reports are completed within 2 days after the inspection, and the report will be emailed to you.

When you receive the report, read it, and write down your concerns. Your home inspector should have given thorough explanations and taken plenty of pictures so you can easily understand the report. Ask your real estate advisor or the home inspector to answer your questions.

Together, you and your REALTOR® will identify the items you want the seller to fix. Your agent will prepare a repair request form and send it to the seller's agent. Note that the seller is NOT required to fix anything, but you can certainly ask. You can request the seller to either fix the items, give you a credit, or lower the purchase price.

Remember, the repair request is another point of negotiation that can work in your favor!

Reports Must Be Completed within Timeframe Required by your Offer

The home inspection report, the pest control report, and any other inspections must be completed within the timeframe required by your offer.

Your purchase contract may have a standard contingency period for inspections, or it may be mutually agreed to by both seller and buyer. In some areas, the contingency is known as a "subject to".

Often the mortgage lender will require the pest control report "Section 1" items be fixed. After the repairs are done, the pest control company will issue a Certificate of Completion so the lender can fund your loan. The pest control repairs are usually the seller's responsibility, or as otherwise stated in your purchase offer.

During the Contingency Period, You Can Back Out Without Penalty

During the contingency period, if the results of the home inspection are ugly, and the seller refuses to fix the items or to compensate you, then you can usually back out without penalty. Check with your real estate advisor to verify.

The main reason you want to have your inspection early in the process, and ask the seller to fix items as early as possible, is because this is still a negotiating point. If the home inspection reveals that the house has too many problems for you, or if the seller refuses to fix anything, this could be a deal breaker. If you are within your contract contingency period, you can cancel this transaction and you should be able to get a full refund of your earnest money deposit from the escrow/settlement office.

3. Order Appraisal

What is an appraisal and why is it important? Facts you should know about appraisals.

- An appraisal is an opinion of the home's value
- It is not "fair market value"
- Your mortgage lender requires an appraisal
- Your lender will approve your purchase based on the appraised value
- The appraisal must be completed within the timeframe required by your offer
- If the appraised value of the home is lower than your agreed purchase priced, you can ask the seller to lower the price or you can cancel the contract (assuming the appraisal was a contingency)
- If the appraised value is higher than the agreed purchase price, keep it secret between you and your REALTOR®

Be Prepared to Pay for your Appraisal in Advance

After the loan process gets started, your lender will order an appraisal. An appraisal is a report that estimates how much the house is worth. A licensed appraiser will go to the house, take photos, measure the rooms, and examine the condition of the interior and exterior. The appraiser will research similar comparable properties that sold recently, and use those comps to calculate the value of your new home.

The appraiser's opinion of your home is very important. Your mortgage lender will use that appraisal to determine how much money they will lend you.

Appraisal Must Be Completed within the Offer Timeframe

In your purchase offer, the appraisal value was probably marked as a contingency of your purchase. In other words, you only have a few days for the appraiser to determine your property value before you "sign off" on the final contract. Make sure the appraisal is completed as early in the process as possible. In fact, as soon as you sign your contract for purchase, your mortgage lender should work to get your loan approved and order the appraisal.

Be prepared to pay for your appraisal up front. An appraisal typically costs about $400. Your mortgage lender will collect this fee from you before ordering the appraisal. You are probably wondering: will you be able to receive a refund for the appraisal if you choose not to buy this house? The answer is no. Ordering the appraisal is a risk. That's why you want to make sure that you are ready to purchase this house before moving forward.

What if the Home Appraises Below the Purchase Price?

The appraisal value often matches the exact selling price that the buyer and seller have agreed to. That is because an appraisal estimates the fair market value. When a buyer and a seller in an open market agree to a purchase price, that is a strong indication of the actual market value. Most appraisers will recognize the purchase price as a valuation of the fair market price.

So you may be asking: *what happens if the appraisal comes in lower than our purchase price?* That's a great question. If the property's appraisal value is less than the purchase price, you have agreed to, your mortgage lender may not agree to the purchase. Therefore, you will likely request that the seller lower his purchase price to the appraisal price. In some instances, the buyer can contribute the difference in cash.

For example, you and the seller agree to a purchase price of $270,000. However, the appraised value is only $260,000. Therefore, if you have extra cash, you can simply pay the $10,000 difference. Although, what if you do not have that extra cash? Or if your lender does not allow you to contribute extra cash? Alternatively, what if you do not think the house is worth the extra amount? As I just mentioned, you would ask the seller to lower the price to match the appraised value. If the seller refuses to lower the purchase price, consult with your trusty REALTOR®. You may want to cancel the contract and find a new house to buy. If the appraisal was listed in your purchase contract as a contingency (or "subject to"), you should be able to back out without penalty.

What if the Appraisal is Higher than the Purchase Price?

Now what if the appraised value of the home is higher than your purchase price? Well that means, my friend, you are getting a fabulous bargain! However, keep this little piece of important news between you and your REALTOR®. You don't need to show your appraisal to the seller, and in this case, it is probably best to keep it to yourself. Smile, and be grateful that you were blessed with a great deal!

4. Sign Disclosures

Document, Documents, and More Documents

Do you feel like you are drowning in paperwork right about now? You may be wondering why there are so many disclosures to sign.

- To make sure that all parties are fully informed
- So that the transaction is fair for both the buyer and the seller
- To prevent lawsuits later on
- To comply with state, federal, and local laws

Review and Sign Disclosures Provided by Seller

During the home purchase process, you will sign a lot of paperwork. In particular, there are many, many disclosures. Disclosures are important documents that help to limit liability and prevent lawsuits later on. Your agent can send you the documents to sign electronically on your computer. It makes the process much easier, because you do not have to print out the paperwork. You can simply read the documents and sign them on your computer or your iPad with a "click".

Remember, even if you receive documents electronically, you can still print them out and save paper copies for your files. However, if you really want to save paper, simply ask your REALTOR® to give you a CD with all of your documents at the end of your transaction.

Ask any Questions You May Have

While you are reading and reviewing the documents and the disclosures, you may see some unfamiliar terms. Or, you may have some questions about what the disclosures mean or how they will affect you.

Naturally, your REALTOR® is the person who can answer your questions. Make a list, and then make an appointment time to meet with your agent. Questions regarding real estate processes are difficult to explain and answer via email, so make a phone or in-person appointment to get all of your questions answered. If there are any questions your REALTOR® cannot answer, he or she will direct you to the correct person who will have the knowledge needed to answer your questions.

Review and Complete the Disclosures within the Offer Timeframe

Once again, there is a specific length of time to read and respond to the disclosures. Make sure you complete the disclosures right away, so that if you have any questions or concerns, they can be addressed before you get any further along in the contract. Once you release the contingencies, your purchase contract becomes permanent.

You will receive documents from various sources: your agent, your agent's transaction coordinator, the escrow officer, and your mortgage lender. You (and your husband or wife) should sign and return all documents within 24 hours of receiving them.

5. Review Title Report

Do not buy a home without going through escrow and obtaining title insurance! That may be a very big mistake. Title insurance is important because it guarantees you are receiving clear title and legal ownership to the property.

There are 2 types of title insurance issued: (1) owner's title insurance, which is for the owner selling to the buyer (and insures the buyer against "defects" in title); and (2) lender's title insurance, which insures the mortgage lender against title defects. Obviously if you are paying cash instead of obtaining a mortgage loan, there won't be any lender's title insurance.

The escrow or settlement company will prepare a title report. It is a record of ownership of the property. It details all the rights and restrictions of the owner including:

- Mortgage liens
- Utility easements
- Public right-of-ways
- CC&R restrictions
- Property taxes that are paid or due
- HOA special assessments

If you buy real estate **without** title insurance, (for example buying property with a Quit Claim Deed directly from the seller) you risk having claims made against your title (your right) to the property. And when you attempt to sell the property later on, it could be difficult (or impossible) for the new buyer to obtain title insurance, and therefore they may not buy it. So always get title insurance!

Review the Preliminary Title Report from Escrow

You should receive a preliminary title report soon after escrow is opened. The title report will include things like previous owners of the property, outstanding liens and mortgages, easements and right-of-ways from utility companies, and CC&Rs, (which stands for "covenants, codes, and restrictions") recorded against this property. This report is also referred to as a "Prelim".

If there are problems with the previous title, such as incorrect vesting or erroneous title transfers, the title company will not insure this house. If you cannot get title insurance, then you would not be able to buy this house. Mortgage lenders will not loan money on a property that does not qualify for title insurance. Although it is very rare that a house is uninsurable, it does happen.

Of course, with distressed properties, the homeowners association may have put a lien against the property if the sellers are delinquent on their HOA dues. So review the title report with your REALTOR® if you see unusual items or anything you do not understand.

Complete and Return the Statement of Identity Immediately

Also during this time, the escrow company will collect a statement of identity form (SI) from each buyer and seller. This form is also known as a "Statement of Information". They will examine public records relating to the buyers and sellers, to verify that the parties do not have any outstanding liens that would prevent them from selling or buying.

For example, the seller may have a tax lien from the IRS that must be paid or satisfied before they can sell the property. Another issue that we see frequently is when a buyer has an outstanding child support obligation, and that debt must be settled before close of escrow.

Get Clear Title by Verifying your Identity

All buyers and all sellers must fill out the SI form completely and correctly. This form should be submitted as soon as escrow is opened, so that any issues can be resolved right away and not delay the closing of escrow. I know it can sometimes be annoying to fill out all the paperwork, especially the SI form. It asks about previous jobs, previous residences, prior marriages, and divorces, so you will need to pull documents out of your file cabinet to complete this form. Once you get started filling out the form, it's not too hard. Just do it quick and turn it in right away.

Several times, we have gotten to the closing date and discovered that we cannot close escrow due to a title issue. The issue was from the buyer, the seller, or the property itself. These problems can be prevented by having the escrow and title company identify all potential issues at the beginning of escrow.

Once, the seller had an IRS lien and it was not discovered until the very end of the escrow process. We eventually got the IRS to waive the lien against the property, since it was a short sale and the seller was not receiving any proceeds, but it was really a hassle and took 2 extra weeks.

Another seller had a lien from the HOA. He did not have the money to pay the lien so we had to find a creative way to get it paid. It took 3 extra weeks, and meanwhile the buyer could not close escrow and could not move into his new home.

Another time, the buyer had a child support lien. He had paid it in full, but it took four weeks to get the clearance letter from county district attorney's office. We could not close escrow until the lien status was cleared and verified.

In yet another instance, the title company discovered that a transfer between owners had been done incorrectly five years ago, and so the seller had to contact the previous owners and get them to draw up and sign legal documents. It was challenging because one owner had already passed away.

Thank goodness, we have been able to get most of our escrows closed, even with these types of challenges.

The lesson we learned is to check the title up front and ask the title and escrow company to verify that there would not be any hold-ups.

6. Get Homeowners Insurance

It is important to get a quote for homeowners insurance right away, so that:

- You can figure out your costs and your budget
- Your mortgage lender can calculate your total housing payment and debt ratio
- If there were previous insurance claims against the house, you will find that out sooner rather than later
- If the property is uninsurable, you still have time to cancel your contract
- You can decide if you need additional riders

Call your Insurance Agent to Get a Quote

Next, we are going to order home insurance. It's also referred to as fire insurance or hazard insurance. You probably already have vehicle insurance on your automobile, renter insurance on your furniture and perhaps even life insurance. So give your insurance agent a call, and find out if he or she offers homeowners' insurance for your house. Most likely, you can get a discounted rate by grouping all of your insurance together at the same company.

Make an appointment to meet your insurance agent in person. Go into her office and tell her about your new house. She will need to know the address, the square footage, how many bedrooms and bathrooms, what type of foundation, what type of roof, if it has a fireplace or security system, the number of smoke detectors, and other important features of your home. If you don't know these answers, you can call your REALTOR® to find out.

Get a couple of different options with varying levels of deductibles. Most insurance policies will be paid annually or bi-annually, which is twice per year. Your first year's payment will be paid out of escrow at closing. So you do not have to pay now, you just need to get quotes. If you own a business, ask your insurance agent if umbrella insurance is appropriate for your situation. You want to make sure that all of your assets are protected.

Verify Property Coverage and Insurance Cost

Before your insurance company insures your new home, they will research an insurance database. They will research the property, the buyer, and the seller. They will find out if there were any prior insurance claims against the home. If there were previous claims, the insurance company may decline to insure your home. If they decline to insure the home, you will not be able to buy the home, because your mortgage lender will require you to have insurance coverage.

Another item the insurance company will check is the insurability of the buyer, and possibly even the insurability of the seller. They will check to see how many insurance claims you have filed in the past, or were filed against you.

It is rare that your insurance company will refuse to insure your home, but it does happen. You need to have this conversation with your insurance agent as soon as you have selected your house, and before your contingency period expires, so that if the house is uninsurable you can cancel the contract and receive your earnest money deposit back.

I have learned a lot about insurability of houses through my vast real estate experience. One time, my buyer client was buying a house that had a prior water damage claim for large plumbing leak. They had filed an insurance claim within the last year, so the new insurance company did not want to insure the home.

In another transaction, my buyer was denied insurance for her new home. The insurance company found out that her dog had attacked a neighbor, and the neighbor had filed a claim against her current homeowner's insurance and received a large settlement. Therefore, she was not able to get insurance for her new home.

Don't assume that everything is automatically covered! Many things are excluded, including some catastrophes. If you want additional coverage, above the basic, ask your insurance agent for a rider or endorsement. Besides the basic homeowners / fire insurance, you may want to get additional cover for earthquakes, flood damage, hurricanes, beach and windstorm, or sewer backup. Additional coverage will cost extra, so check with your insurance agent for eligibility and cost.

Give the Insurance Quote to the Escrow Officer

Your insurance agent will give you a quote known as a "binder", and will send that directly to the escrow officer. Once the escrow officer has your homeowners' insurance quote, she will put the estimated costs into the HUD-1 closing calculation and order the "binder" before close of escrow. Your mortgage lender may need a copy of the insurance binder also.

An insurance binder is an insurance policy quote that is ready to go into effect and "bind" the insurance to the property upon close of escrow. It means that your policy is approved by the insurance company and coverage starts before the actual policy begins. Therefore, your coverage can begin the minute you own your home, even though the payment is being mailed to the insurance company and they haven't yet received it. Your insurance agent can give you more details.

7. Final Loan Approval

Well, now you are almost to the finish line. Just a few more hurdles to jump over. So keep going strong!

Your mortgage lender will probably ask you for more paperwork shortly before closing, so be ready to give him documents right away. Here are a few documents you will probably see:

- LOE: letter of explanation (all-purpose form)
- VOI: verification of income
- VOE: verification of employment
- VOR: verification of rent paid
- VOF: verification of funds

In our book, we refer to your home loan as a "mortgage". However, in some states such as California, you will actually sign a Deed of Trust along with a Promissory Note. Your documents may not use the term "mortgage" but for all practical purposes, it's the same. That's why we use the term "mortgage" throughout this book.

Your Lender will Approve You for your Loan

During this time, your lender will finalize the loan and approve both the property and you (as the borrower) for the loan. The mortgage lender has to go through several phases, including DU (desktop underwriting) approval. The underwriting department will review the loan documents and the appraisal and ask for many details.

Once you have your loan approval, you are in position to close escrow. Congratulations! That is an important hurdle to jump. Loan approvals take a lot of work, so stick with the process until you get your approval letter. That is something of which to be proud.

Stay in Touch with your Lender to Ensure the Loan Closes on Time

Your mortgage loan will drive the closing process. The lender has to fund your loan before closing; and before your loan can be funded, you must sign loan documents; and, before you can sign loan documents, their underwriting department must underwrite the loan. Before the underwriting department will approve your loan, they must examine all of your documents and you must meet their strict criteria.

It is important to stay in touch with your lender every step of the way. Call him every 2 days to see if he needs any documents from you.

Provide Requested Additional Documents Promptly

Any time your lender asks you for additional documents, provide them immediately or you could delay the escrow closing (and be penalized).

If your mortgage lender asks you to submit documents or to fill out any forms, please provide those right away. By cooperating promptly, it helps the lender get his or her job done on time, which also means that your closing will be done on time.

If you fail to provide the necessary documents, your lender may not be able to fund the mortgage loan on time. If the escrow is delayed, you may have to pay penalties. The penalties may be imposed by the seller, the seller's short sale lender, or by your lender.

Yes, I know it is annoying that you have to provide so much paperwork, but it is a part of the process. Just get it done quickly with a positive, grateful attitude!

8. Plan Your Moving Date

Earlier, we talked about starting to plan for your move-out. Now it's time to start moving. The best way to plan your moving date:

- Give your landlord a 30 or 60-day notice in writing
- Arrange for friends or a moving company to help you
- Plan to move about 2 weeks AFTER your closing date

Since You Made it this Far, it is Safe to Plan your Moving Date

Whew! Okay, so we made it past the loan documents and now are ready to plan our moving date. A few steps ago, we discussed starting to plan for utilities, mail change, and giving a notice to your landlord. Now let's plan our actual moving date. Hurray! We are going to put a date on the calendar and start planning around that date. However, of course, we will still be flexible because we know the date may change.

Give your Landlord your Notice to Move

It is time to give your landlord your 30 or 60-day notice to move IN WRITING. Even if you did not like the home or your landlord, be respectful and polite at all times. Remember, your landlord gave you a good renter reference that helped you qualify for your loan to buy your house. Your landlord will continue to be a good reference for you in the future.

Remember: Never burn bridges behind you. Instead, develop good business relationships by giving your notice legally in writing.

By giving 30 or 60 days advance notice, paying your rent current, and thoroughly cleaning the house when you move out, you will leave a legacy of goodwill. Your landlord will appreciate you, support you, and be happy for your new home. You will feel better about yourself when you follow procedures correctly and fairly for everyone involved.

Arrange for a Moving Company to Help You Move

If you hired a moving company, now's the time to call and get on their schedule. Remember, they are often booked up in advance. Do you want them to pack your boxes and wrap your furniture before moving? Of course, this does cost extra, but your time is valuable. Maybe you want to save money by packing the boxes yourself.

If you are not hiring a moving company, call your best friends — the people you know you can count on — and ask them to put your moving date on their calendar. Even if you rent a U-Haul® and do it yourself, you are going to need some strong guys to help with the big furniture and heavy boxes.

Make it fun by throwing a pizza party or BBQ for your friends after the move is done. Even though they are happy to support you, a little touch of thoughtfulness shows your appreciation for your friends who took the time and effort to help you.

Overlap Occupancy to Eliminate Stress

Earlier, we discussed overlapping your occupancy. What exactly does that mean? Well, it means you would continue renting your current home for a couple of weeks after you own your new home. Why would you want to overlap? Since you need some time to move from one house to another without stress. If possible, you should take a few days off of work in order to move. But even then, moving can be stressful.

We suggest overlapping because it makes your move smoother and hassle-free. It is good to have a small cushion just in case escrow does not close on the day you planned, and that does happen sometimes. If your REALTOR® calls and says that your closing will be delayed by a couple of days, you can still relax knowing that you will be ready, either way!

STEP 8: Closing Escrow

In Chapter 8, we are nearing the end of our home buying process. Once you know that your home purchase is going to close, there are things you will need to do and some things you should NOT do. We will discuss how to find services in your new neighborhood, and what NOT to buy before close of escrow. You have wrapped up the final details for the close of escrow, signed your loan documents, paid your final closing costs, and have received keys to your new home. Here is what we're going to do next.

1. Find neighborhood services and change your mailing address
2. Don't buy new furniture
3. Inspect the house
4. Review closing documents
5. Review loan docs
6. Sign loan docs
7. Pay your closing costs
8. Wire loan funds
9. Get utilities connected
10. Pick up your keys

1. Find Neighborhood Services

You're going to need to make "new friends" in your new neighborhood! That includes your new banker, your new postman, and your new grocery store clerk. Just like you had favorite places to shop, to dine, and to play in your old neighborhood, you'll need to make new connections here in your new community.

Mail Change of Address Form

Now it is time to submit a change of address to the post office. Remember, it will be important for your mail to follow you to your new home. You can go online at *www.USPS.com* and complete a change of address form. Although you can submit the form online, sometimes it is not processed correctly, so it is better to take it to the post office in person.

In addition to notifying the post office, you should notify people and vendors who send you mail. Most of your vendors will allow you to go online and complete a change of address request. Remember to notify your state driver's license and vehicle registration department. And don't forget your voter registration! Note that the USPS forwarding is only valid for 6 months, and after that, your mail sent to the old address will be returned back to the sender. You don't want to miss that critical mail!

It is very important that you notify your utility companies of your new address. They will send you a final bill, and expect you to pay it right away. If not, they will send your account to collections, and you will get a ding on your credit. Many utility companies, including the phone company, are quick to turn over your account to collections after you close your account. Within a matter of 2 months, you could already have a negative item on your credit without knowing it. You have worked hard to get and keep good credit, so be sure to follow up and pay your closing utility statements.

Also, be cooperative with the seller, and if any of his mail accidently comes to your new address, notify him right away. Hopefully, the family that moves into your previous rental home will do the same for you!

Make Arrangements for Services in your New Neighborhood

If you are moving to a new area you will need to open or transfer your bank accounts, apply to school for your children, church, and community activities.

In your new neighborhood, you have probably already selected schools for your children. Your children will be assigned to schools based on their grade level and your new address. You probably won't get to select your favorite school. However, if you have done your homework, you already took this factor into consideration when house-hunting.

You will need to go to the school district office and complete an application for your children to enroll at the new school. The school will ask you for proof of your new address, so you can show them a copy of your purchase contract. They will also ask you for a copy of your child's birth certificate and proof of immunization records, so be prepared with the correct paperwork.

You may want to open a bank account at your local bank in your new neighborhood. If you are moving far away from your old home, you may be looking for a new church or place of worship. There is bound to be a congregation near your new home.

Lastly, find out what type of community activities are going on in your new neighborhood. Especially important are the recreational activities that the entire family can enjoy, such as a park within walking distance.

2. Do Not Buy New Furniture!

Do not purchase anything on your credit while you are going through the loan process. Do NOT spend your money from your savings account, which is your down payment.

Do NOT Purchase New Furniture, Electronics, or Appliances!

Earlier, we discussed one of the biggest mistakes that new homebuyers sometimes make. A homebuyer may get so excited about her new home, that she will purchase furniture or appliances for the new home. Perhaps the homebuyer wants new electronics, such as a TV, computer, or stereo system in his new home. That's the biggest mistake a homebuyer could make!

Buying Items on Credit can Ruin your Mortgage Loan Approval

How would you like to have new furniture, brand new appliances, a new flat-screen TV, and yet have no house to put them in? That would be very disappointing, wouldn't it. That is what could happen if you jeopardize your loan by making purchases on credit BEFORE you close escrow. It is easy to get excited, but wait until AFTER you move in to buy anything new.

Your Lender will Check your Credit Again

You probably were not aware of this, but a few days before closing, your mortgage lender will pull your credit report again. He will verify that your credit is still the same as it was when you applied for the loan. If additional items show up on your credit report, such as a new account you applied for, it could change your loan approval.

If a new credit account shows up on your report, the lender will ask you to write a letter called LOE, which stands for letter of explanation. If you were approved for the new credit account, the lender will recalculate your debt ratio to include your new debt, which means your debt may now be too high to qualify for your mortgage loan.

Save your Cash for Closing Costs

You need to keep your priorities in mind. Your first priority is to get your home purchase closed and get the keys in your hand. Your next priority is to make sure that you can afford to pay the mortgage each month. Don't jeopardize your dream home!

3. Inspect the House

Why should you walk through the house and inspect it a few days before closing?

- To ensure the seller has completed any repairs you requested
- To ensure that the physical condition of the property is the same as before you opened escrow
- To take measurements for moving your furniture in
- To sign off approval of the property condition

A few days before closing, it's important for you to physically walk through the property. This visual inspection will simply verify that the home is in the same condition as when you originally viewed it, except the items the seller fixed. If not, you **cannot** simply back out of the transaction, but you can delay escrow closing until the seller corrects the items. For example, the seller agreed to remove the debris from the backyard and the trash is still there. So your agent must send a written removal request to the seller's agent.

Visit the House AFTER the Seller Completes Repairs

After you reviewed the home inspection, if you found repairs that you wanted the seller to fix, your REALTOR® prepared a repair request form and sent it to the seller. If the seller agreed to fix these items, it is important for you to inspect the house and verify that the work was completed.

You will have the opportunity physically to inspect the house several days before closing. Your REALTOR® will schedule this inspection with the other agent. You will want to make sure that the house is vacant and in good condition as you expected.

Remember, the seller is not obligated to clean the house. So don't expect the house to be squeaky clean. It will be your responsibility to clean it upon moving in.

Take your checklist with the repair items and look to make sure each item was fixed. Consider paying the home inspector to come back and re-inspect items to verify they were repaired properly.

In addition, you should ask for receipts from the seller's contractor. Then you can determine if the work was performed by a licensed contractor, a handyman, or the sellers.

Is the Property Condition the Same as Before?

One of the most important reasons to perform a walk-through of the house is to make sure that nothing has substantially changed. Verify that all of the appliances you asked for are still in the house. Anything else you asked for in the contract should remain in the house also. Look around and make sure there was no major damage when the residents moved out. For example, if they removed the refrigerator, washer, or dryer, verify that the floor was not scuffed during the move.

If you asked the seller to remove personal property, such as a satellite dish or a workbench, make sure that the seller took these items with him. Also, walk around the yard and make sure the seller did not leave any debris in the yard. You do not need to test the appliances or anything else. This is simply a visual walk-through. If the home is not in the condition that you expect, you need to let your REALTOR® know right away so she can talk to the other agent and request that the seller correct things.

At this point, it is too late to cancel your contract. However, you can address issues with the seller to make things right, or to give you a small credit if not. Perhaps the seller was going to leave the refrigerator, but now you see it is gone. You didn't buy a refrigerator because you were depending on it coming with the house. Your REALTOR® may ask the seller to give you a $200 credit to purchase a refrigerator similar to the one that was in the home when you first viewed it.

Sign off Approval of the Property Condition

When the buyers do their final walk-through, they sign a form to verify its condition. Here in California, we call it a VP form, which stands for verification of property condition. Both real estate agents also perform a visual inspection of the house and make notes on its condition. That is done using the Agent Visual Inspection Disclosure (AVID) form. Both you and your REALTOR® can perform your inspections at the same time.

While you are there at the property, look at the rooms and sketch out a diagram. Measure the rooms with a tape measure so that you can decide where to place your furniture before you move in. You may find that some of your furniture is too large to fit into your new house or you have too much furniture. Measuring in advance will help you to determine what furniture you need to get rid of before you move. This could save you the trouble of moving furniture into your new home that would not fit.

4. Review Closing Docs

You should review the Estimated Closing Statement with your REALTOR® before the closing date because you want to:

- Verify that all the charges are correct
- Ensure that you are prepared to pay your costs before closing

The Escrow Company Prepares a Closing Statement

Now, you are going to review your closing documents. There is the HUD-1, which we have included as a sample form. It is a complex document, difficult to read and understand. You can ask the escrow company for their own version of the estimated statement of closing costs. We have included a sample of that form as well. It is much easier to read and to understand. You can quickly scan the form to find out what your charges are and see your bottom line. This form is called an Estimated Statement of Closing Costs.

Review Closing Documents with your REALTOR®

Verify all the charges are correct and ensure that you are prepared to pay your costs before closing. Your REALTOR® can review this form with you and explain it. If you don't understand some of the escrow or title fees, you can also call your escrow/settlement officer. If you have questions about the mortgage loan fees, you should call your mortgage lender and get your loan questions answered.

On this form, you will see the charges that are due and how much money you will have to pay before closing. This is an important figure because you want to make sure that you have enough money to pay these closing costs. Once you have paid your down payment and closing costs, then your bottom line may be a refund that you will receive after closing.

5. Review Loan Docs

You need to make sure that everything is correct on the paperwork. Remember, real people type these documents, and so clerical errors and typos do happen sometimes. For example,

I once saw a loan document package and all the names of the borrowers were spelled wrong. This does not happen very often; but when it does, your documents will need to be corrected before the actual signing date.

For instance, if you were at your loan document signing appointment, and the documents were wrong, you would not be able to sign your documents that day. It takes about 2 days to re-draw new loan documents and that would delay your closing date by 2 extra days.

Review the Borrower's Loan Docs Before your Loan Signing Appointment

Since you have been working hand-in-hand with your mortgage lender and developed a good working relationship with him, ask him to send you a copy of your loan document package prior to your loan signing appointment. It is important to get these loan documents in advance because there are so many pages and the paperwork can be a little bit complex.

Review Docs and Write Down Questions for your Lender

There can be more than 100 pages to review and sign. That's why we recommend receiving a copy of the loan documents in advance so you have time to read each document thoroughly. When you have a question, put a bright sticky note on each page that you need clarified.

Get your Questions Answered Before your Signing

When you are finished reviewing the documents, call your lender and get all your questions answered. Once you feel confident that you have all your questions answered, you can go to your loan signing appointment and it will be a breeze!

6. Sign Loan Docs

Now that you know what documents to expect as a part of your mortgage loan and you've gotten all of your questions answered, it is time to sign the loan documents.

How to prepare when you sign the loan documents:

- Have a notary public present to notarize your signatures
- Bring your driver's licenses or legal proof of identification
- Do NOT bring your children
- Schedule about 1.5 to 2 hours of time (less time if you have already reviewed the docs in advance)

NOTE: If you are in a "table-funding" state, this may be done at the closing table instead of in advance.

Sign Loan Docs at Escrow before the Scheduled Closing Date

Shortly before your closing date, you will need to sign loan documents before a Notary Public. This often happens about 2 days before close of escrow, depending on your region's customs. Every borrower who is signing the loan documents will need to be present. The loan document signing appointment may take place during the workday; and if so, you will need to take a few hours off from work.

You will need to meet your Notary Public in a quiet office without any distractions. The Notary must be focused on the correct legal procedures to ensure that everything is signed correctly and your loan documents are notarized properly. This is an important procedure and you will need ample time to review and sign all the paperwork. If the documents are not signed correctly, they will have to be re-done and that would delay your closing by several days.

Take your Driver's Licenses for Proof of Identification

You will need to bring your driver's licenses or legal proof of identification. Ladies, if you have married recently and changed your last name, you may need to bring more than 1 type of identification. If your driver's license has your maiden name instead of your new married last name, you will need to show proof of your new last name in a legal format that is acceptable to the Notary Public.

Do NOT bring your children. Your children will not be able to attend the loan document signing appointment. You will need to find suitable childcare in advance.

Expect to Spend at Least 1.5 hours Signing Documents

The loan document signing appointment takes an average of 1.5 hours from start to finish. If you have the opportunity to review your loan documents in advance and get all of your questions answered, your appointment can be as short as 45 minutes. If you do not have the opportunity to read your documents in advance, your appointment may take 2 hours or more because you will want to read the documents, and you may have questions.

Another tip is to make sure your mortgage lender will be available to answer questions during your loan document signing. Even if your lender cannot be present in person, he should be available by phone. By this time, you probably already have your lender programmed into your phone on speed dial!

There May Be Over 50 pages to Initial and Sign

The average loan document package has 100 or more page, and you may be signing or initialing 50 of those pages. You need to be able to concentrate on reviewing and signing each document properly. If you received the loan package in advance, bring it with you as it may answer questions at the signing appointment.

At the end of your appointment, the Notary will review all the documents for signatures and initials, but she CANNOT explain documents, advise you, or give legal opinions. That is why you need your lender to be available to answer your questions.

7. Pay Your Closing Costs

NOTE: In California, we close escrow about 2 days after loan funding. However, other states have "table funding" where all parties gather around the closing table as the loan document signing, loan funding, and closing happens all at once.

Bring your Final Down Payment to Escrow

I hope you have not spent your hard-earned money just yet, because now it is time to deposit your final down payment and pay your loan closing fees. About 2 days before the scheduled closing date, you will have to deposit your final down payment (if any) and pay your loan closing fees. Check with your REALTOR® or your escrow/settlement officer and find out exactly how much money you need to bring in.

Take your Certified Funds to Escrow

Be sure to take certified funds into the escrow/settlement company or attorney's office. Certified funds means a cashier's check or a certified bank check. They will not accept cash or personal checks. The funds should be made payable to the escrow or the settlement company. Be sure to get a receipt. If you send the funds via wire transfer from your bank, call your escrow company to verify the bank routing info first.

8. Wire Loan Funds

Depending on the process for your state, your completed loan documents will be reviewed by several people. Who may be reviewing your documents before your loan is funded?

- Notary Public
- Escrow Officer
- Mortgage underwriter
- Mortgage funder

The Escrow Officer Forwards the Signed Loan Docs to the Lender

After you have signed the loan documents, the escrow officer (or the settlement officer) will review the loan documents. She will pull out the closing documents that stay with the escrow company, and forward the mortgage document package to your lender.

You will also receive the documents package for your files. Put the package in a file folder so you can refer to them later. You will have already started a file with your house hunting paperwork. Just add these loan documents into your home purchase file folder and keep the file in a safe place.

The Lender Wires Loan Funds to Escrow

After the escrow officer (or settlement officer) reviews the loan documents, she will forward them to your lender. His underwriter will review the signed documents.

If the underwriter approves the documents, she will forward them to the funder. He will then review the documents and if he approves them, he will wire your loan money to the escrow company.

"Funding" is a critical step for closing. Without the funds, you cannot close escrow. The entire closing phase is dependent upon the mortgage loan funding, which is the "green light" to close escrow. Once your loan is funded, you can breathe a sigh of relief. The last major hurdle is over!

Closing Date Finalized

By this time, you will know whether escrow will be closing on time, and if not, when to expect the closing. You are so close to becoming a homeowner! If all of the documents are signed correctly, you will know when your mortgage lender wires funds for your home purchase. If all of the steps happened on time, you probably will close escrow on time. However, if there was a delay in the steps, your closing will be delayed also.

Stay in touch with your real estate agent, your mortgage lender, and your escrow/settlement officer throughout the closing phase.

9. Get Utilities Connected

Whew! Your loan was funded and now you need to get the utilities connected so you can move in. The utility companies will require security deposits to turn on the power and water service. Some utility companies do not require a deposit if you show you have good credit. Others may refund your deposit back to you if you paid your bills on time for a certain number of months.

Schedule the Utilities Turned on at your New Home

Now that you know you are moving into your new home very soon, you don't want to move into a dark home. Even though you have some overlap with your old home, and you may not be living in your new home right away, you will need the utilities turned on in order to begin moving. Be sure to contact the following utility companies: water/sewer, trash, gas or fuel, electric power, cable or internet, and phone (optional landline).

You will need the utilities turned on soon because you will need electricity to see your moving boxes. Connect the water right away so you can use the bathroom while unpacking your new home.

You may have to pay a deposit on your new utilities. The deposit may be $200 or more. It is a good thing you saved up your money because you are going to need to have water, power, and fuel in your new home. If you have good credit, you may not have to pay a deposit. Oftentimes, if you pay your utility bill on time for a while, you will get a refund of your security deposit.

Avoid a Reconnection Fee

If you already have utilities in your name with the same utility companies, you can simply ask for a transfer of service. Since you have paid your previous utility bill on time, the company will be happy to establish a new service for you in a new location. It is okay to have overlapping service on multiple homes. So if possible, transfer the utilities to your new home before the seller shuts them off.

If you can get your service connected before the seller turns off his utilities, you can often save money. That is because the utility company can simply switch the service into your name by taking a meter reading on the date of transfer. However, if they have to come out, shut off the utility, and then have to make a second trip to turn it back on again, they will charge you a reconnection fee and that will cost more money.

10. Pick Up Your Keys!

This is the moment you've been waiting for: *The keys to your new home!*

Your REALTOR® Notifies You that Deed is Now Recorded

On the day of the closing, your REALTOR® will contact you when your new deed is recorded at the county clerk recorder's office. It means that the house is now legally yours! This is a time of great joy for you and your family.

Arrange to Pick up the Key from your REALTOR®

Your REALTOR® will meet you to give you your key to your new home. You will receive multiple keys, along with garage door remote "clickers", mailbox keys, shed keys, and gate remote entry "clickers" if the home is in a gated community. In certain communities, you will need to pick up your mailbox keys from the post office, and they require you to pay a deposit.

Get your Keys at the Closing Table

If you are buying a home in a state that operates on the "closing table" concept, your REALTOR® may hand you your keys after sign the documents at the closing table.

Great job, escrow is now closed and the home is yours.

STEP 9: Your New Home

Now you have your new home and it is all yours. Congratulations! This is a very exciting day, but there are a few more things we need to take care of first.

In this step we are going to talk about moving into your home, showing thanks to your vendors, how to take care of your new home, and, most importantly, financial management. This step has many little tips to help finish the process of home purchase and get you started on the right path of being a terrific homeowner.

1. Congratulations!

You now know FOR SURE that you will be moving into your home. The emotional roller coaster and the uncertainty are over. The ups and downs of home buying are now replaced with joy and relief.

You Are Now the Proud Owner of your Own Home

Well done! You have just purchased your first home. This is a very thrilling experience. You have learned about the process of real estate and you are now ready and prepared to take on the responsibility of caring for your first home.

> *"Build up equity in your home and invest your home dividends wisely. If you do, your home will be the best investment you will ever make."*
> *p.189 (Smith, 2008)*

At this point, you and your family and friends are probably jumping for joy. Maybe you never thought you would see this day. You were dreaming, hoping, and praying for years to reach this goal of home ownership. You have a lot to celebrate. Be proud of yourself for setting your goal and following through and not letting obstacles stop you from reaching your dream of homeownership.

You can Breathe a Sigh of Relief

Besides being excited, you are probably very relieved. There may have been some days when you were uncertain that you would reach your goal. You persevered and kept stepping forward. You can breathe a big sigh of relief that you have fulfilled your dream and now you will enjoy being a homeowner!

2. Call the Movers

Why did you plan for a 2-week overlap of occupancy between your old and new homes?

- Your home purchase probably will NOT close escrow on exactly the date you plan
- Eliminate stress if the closing date is delayed
- You will need plenty of time to pack and move

It is time to call the movers. You have already reserved a moving truck rental or you have made arrangements with your favorite moving company. Now, contact the moving company to confirm the date and time of your move. When you called the company before, you may have given them a tentative date. Now you can confirm your "for sure" date.

Your Boxes are Already Packed and Labeled

Throughout the home purchase process, you have been packing boxes, labeling them, getting rid of furniture and household goods, and maybe even taking items into storage. Moving is a big process, so you probably have more things to pack and more boxes to label. If so, you will have some excitement from your new home purchase that gives you enough energy to finish packing and moving. Be careful not to get too exhausted. Remember to take a break every once in a while.

Finish Transferring Utilities

Although you have turned on the utilities at your new house, what about the utilities you still have connected in your name at your old house? Finish transferring the utilities. Make sure they are canceled at your old house on the day you will be moving out. If you accidentally leave the utilities on at your old house, the new tenants may start using the utilities and you will have to pay the bill because it is still in your name.

Pack and Move Smoothly and Stress-Free

If you took our advice and you planned for a 2-week overlap in occupancy between your old home and your new home, you will be very happy that you did. Even if your escrow closing was delayed by a week, you still have 1 week of overlap. Assuming you and your family go to work and school during the week, you still have 1 full weekend to finish moving.

Sometimes people have to move for reasons that are unpleasant, such as job loss, death, or divorce. Today you are moving for a very happy reason: because you bought your new dream home! Even though your move is a momentous occasion, filled with joy and excitement, moving can be exhausting. Stay aware of your emotions and be careful to treat your family (and the people helping you move) with kindness and courtesy.

3. Appreciate Your Service Providers

Many business professionals worked hand-in-hand with you as a partner. Why did they do it? Many vendors in the real estate industry really enjoy helping buyers like you. They get great delight when they can help a family like yours move into their new home.

Thank the Professionals who Made your New Home Possible

Many service providers made the purchase of your new home possible. Yes, they were paid, but in the real estate industry, often times they perform a lot of work without being paid. It is nice that they closed escrow successfully and were paid.

However, for your REALTOR®, the icing on the cake is having YOU as a happy first-time homebuyer. Your REALTOR® worked hard just so she could see you smiling with joy. Let your REALTOR® know how much you appreciated his help.

Remember that although your REALTOR® was paid, you probably did not have to pay him a penny. In most cases, the seller paid the buyer's agent. It was a bonus to you that the seller paid both real estate commissions — and isn't that something to be grateful for?

A Successful Home Purchase Takes Effort from Many Parties

You just completed a major life event that took hard work and effort from lots of folks. Who was there for you? Your REALTOR®, mortgage lender, escrow officer, home inspector, notary public, and others. Consider sending these professionals a thank-you card to show your appreciation. It makes their efforts so much more worthwhile when they know it put a smile on your face.

Refer your Friends

A few great ways to thank your REALTOR® and other team partners are:

- Refer your friends and family members
- Write a good recommendation on LinkedIn
- Have a housewarming party and introduce your REALTOR® to your friends

Be sure to refer your friends and family members. Because the greatest compliment that you can give your agent would be a referral. Small business owners and independent contractors depend on word-of-mouth referrals to feed their livelihood. Team partners who served you in an awesome way would appreciate your recommendations and referrals to new clients.

A great review on LinkedIn is always appropriate. Go to the professional networking site *www.linkedin.com* and find your REALTOR®'s profile. You may have already connected with her on the web site, and if so, you are ready to write a great recommendation for her. Linkedin is free to join, and once you join, you can connect with business people.

Throw a House Warming Party

After you move in, decorate, and are settled into your new home, what is the first thing you do? Well of course, you invite your friends to come and enjoy your new home along with you! When you plan your house warming party, be sure to invite your REALTOR® and your mortgage lender to come along and meet your friends. It is a great way to show thanks by introducing them to new prospective clients.

Your REALTOR® may offer to host your house warming event. At our real estate company, we coordinate house warmings for our first-time home buyers after they move in.

First, we give the family time to get their furniture moved in, boxes unpacked, and decorating done. Then we get a list of the seller's friends and family members and send out invitations.

On the invites, we use address labels we have ordered with the homeowner's new address. We coordinate the party set-up and order the food.

On the day of the event, we arrive early and tie balloons outside. Then we greet all the guests and help welcome them to the new home.

4. Give Thanks

Make it a habit to cultivate an attitude of thankfulness. You cannot always change your situation, but you CAN change the way you view it. If you take time to appreciate what you do have — your family, your friends, and your opportunities — you'll have a richer, more satisfying life.

A Prayer of Thanks Comes from a Grateful Heart

Opening the front door with your own key and walking into your home for the first time is an incredible moment that you will remember forever. If you and your family are people of faith, give thanks to God for making your dream possible. Never take success for granted. If ever there was a time for rejoicing, praising, and worshipping, this is that moment!

Many new homeowners will take a moment in their new house to kneel with a prayer of thanks and dedicate their new home to God, who made this home possible for their family.

> *When we moved into our new home, we invited our pastor and his wife to come and pray over our house. With anointing oil, we anointed every room, doorway, hallway, and window. We feel very strongly that we want the Holy Spirit to live in our hearts and our home.*
>
> *We were immensely humbled and we felt so blessed and honored to receive such a gracious gift of a new home. We want every person who comes into our house to be richly blessed also.*

An Attitude of Gratitude goes a Long Way

You enjoy life more when you appreciate what you have. When you have gratitude, you are more likely to take care of the things with which you have been entrusted and you can encourage others with your positive attitude. You'll be happier, your family will be more content, and you will all enjoy a richer life when you have grateful hearts.

5. Take Care of the House

At the beginning of this guide, we discussed why homeowners are more responsible than renters. Now that you're a homeowner, you are ready to take on those responsibilities and take good care of your new home.

As soon as you get the keys, conduct an orientation of your new home. Make sure you know which keys unlock what, that the garage door opener actually opens the garage, and how to turn off the utilities in case of emergency.

<u>Here's a checklist to keep you on track:</u>

- ❑ Test all the locks and keys
- ❑ Garage door opener
- ❑ Gate codes / remotes
- ❑ Common area entry keys (such as swimming pool gate)
- ❑ Mailbox key
- ❑ Smoke detectors & test
- ❑ Carbon monoxide detector & test
- ❑ Water shut-off valve & tool
- ❑ Gas/fuel shut-off valve & tool
- ❑ Circuit breaker for power shut off/on

❑ Sewer clean-out

Neighborhoods with high rates of ownership are more stable, have less crime and better schools. Why? Because home owners **CARE**. They have a vested interest in their community.

Important things you can do to take care of your new home include:

- Regular preventive maintenance to avoid things from breaking
- Repair things immediately when they break
- Get electrical and plumbing done by a professional
- Keep it clean and organized

Maintain Items and Replace Things as They Wear Out

Some household things need regular cleaning and maintenance, while other things will need to be replaced every so often. The good news is that with regular maintenance and attention to details, you can avoid major disasters.

For example, watch your water heater for signs of failure when it is at the end of its life span. Consider replacing it before it fails. You will avoid having the water heater suddenly flood your house or garage with water.

Items that require regular maintenance include:

❑ Check and replace the batteries in the smoke detectors and carbon monoxide detector
❑ Rake the yard and mow the lawn
❑ Weed the flower gardens
❑ Trim the trees and hedges
❑ Clean the fireplace flue
❑ Check the roof and conduct repairs after a major storm
❑ Clear the gutters and roof for leaves
❑ Check the air conditioner
❑ Clean the swimming pool or spa
❑ Clean the heater vents
❑ Replace the heater filters
❑ Clean the clothes dryer vent

Items that wear out and need to be replaced (with approximate lifespan):

❑ Light bulbs and light fixtures (1- 10 years)
❑ Appliances (5 – 20 years)
❑ Faucets (2 – 15 years)
❑ Wood fence, deck, porch, and stairs (10 years)
❑ Toilet guts (10 to 20 years)
❑ Water heater (15 to 20 years)
❑ Furnace (30 years)
❑ Wood siding (30 years)
❑ Roof (25 to 40 years or more)

You will not always have the money to fix big items, such as the roof, which costs thousands of dollars, so put aside money every month into a home repair fund. That way, when you have a big expense, you won't have to take it out of your mortgage budget.

Another thing we should mention for older homes: Eventually, you will have to replace items such as outdated plumbing, older electrical, and inefficient windows. You can do a little bit each year and eventually bring your home up to modern standards.

When Items Break, Repair them Right Away

You know "Murphy's Law": anything that can go wrong, will go wrong. When you are least expecting it, something will break, and if you don't get it fixed right away, it could lead to other problems. That's where your home warranty comes in handy. Most things will be covered and all you will have to pay is a small co-payment, so there is no reason to procrastinate fixing things.

Hire Professionals to do Electrical Work and Plumbing Repairs

<u>TIP</u>: *Always use licensed, bonded contractors who are trust worthy*.

Check their references before hiring building professionals, and get your receipts in writing. If you do any major improvements, you will need to get a permit from your city's building department. A quality contractor will know how to get permits, but you should also verify the permits with the city or county.

This Home is your Children's Future

You want to keep your home in great condition. It is where you live now and where your family can live for many future generations. It is your family's biggest investment, so treasure it and take good care of your home. Even if you move to a bigger home later, you can keep this first home as a real estate investment. Your home is the start of your family legacy.

6. Home Warranty

"It's better to have it and not need it, than to need it, but not have it." Your home warranty is like an insurance policy. The home warranty company will send a repairman to fix things when they break, so you do not have to pay out of pocket with a lot of cash. A home warranty will keep unexpected bills low, and help keep your monthly expenses predictable and manageable.

Just remember Murphy's Law: If you have the home warranty, you probably will not need it, but if you don't have a home warranty, that is when something will break!

Read your Home Warranty

If you followed our recommendation, you received a free home warranty at the close of escrow courtesy of the seller. Be sure to read the policy thoroughly. It covers most things, but not everything.

You can continue renewing the policy each year if you like the service. Since it is a 1 year policy, plan to pay for the next year's policy before it expires.

Put the Warranty Company Phone # on the Fridge

Keep your policy information and phone number handy by sticking it to the side of your refrigerator. "Who you gonna call?" they say in the movies. One call to your home warranty company does it all. They already have a rolodex of screened, licensed contractors who are ready to fix your leaky pipe or the refrigerator that just stopped working.

Remember There is a Small Co-Payment

Home warranty co-payments range may be approximately $60 for a service call. That is much more affordable than coughing up $3,000 for a new furnace in the middle of a cold winter, isn't it?

7. Pay Your Mortgage

Your mortgage and housing expenses are your #1 priority and more important than your other bills, especially consumer goods.

Your homeowner housing expenses include:

- Mortgage (due monthly)
- Property taxes (due twice per year)
- Hazard insurance (due annually)
- HOA fees (if applicable)

Stop and think about it. What is your most important bill? What expenses should be paid first, above all others? Your housing expense should always be paid before anything else because it is the roof over your head. It provides shelter for you and your family. It is the most basic necessity.

- If you don't pay your mortgage (or rent), where are you going to live? So do not jeopardize the security of your family's home. Always make sure your housing bill is paid on the first day of the month, before any other bills are paid.

Pay your Mortgage on Time every Month

You received a mortgage payment coupon when signing your loan documents. You can use that temporary statement to send in your first mortgage payment. After that, your statement will arrive in the mail each month. Your mortgage statement will include things such as the amount due, your previous payment, your interest rate, how much is being collected each month for taxes and insurance, and where to send your payment.

If you used a local lender, as we recommended, you can simply take your mortgage statement into their office when you have questions. If you did not use a local lender, you can call their office to get your questions answered.

Pay your Homeowners Insurance, Property Taxes, and HOA Fees

Many mortgage lenders will collect money from you for the property taxes and the homeowners insurance. They will calculate how much your annual fees and then bill you for 1/12 of that amount with each monthly payment. You pay it with your regular monthly payment, and it is then applied to an "escrow" account or an "impound" account. Your lender would then be in charge of making sure your property taxes and homeowners insurance are paid on time each year.

> *"It is also necessary to carry homeowner's insurance because most of your possessions are stored in your home. If you do not carry homeowner's insurance, you may not have the financial resources available to replace your personal items or rebuild your home if damage or total loss occurs. If disaster strikes, you could be left homeless and in serious debt." p.9 (Rowley, 2007)*

If you send in extra money with your mortgage payment each month, make sure it gets applied to the PRINCIPAL and you will pay off your loan faster! Even if you make one extra payment per year and apply that extra 13th payment entirely to the principal, you may cut up to 7 or more years off of the end of your loan.

Additional Property Tax Bills and HOA Bills

In addition to your regular property taxes assessed from the county government, there may be some "special assessments" included. These are additional fees that must be paid. For example; school bonds or water district improvements which were passed in the local election.

Also be aware that an HOA may also have additional assessments: fees charged for a specific period of time to pay for capital improvement projects such as re-paving the streets, which may only be completed every 10 years. After you close escrow, don't be surprised if the HOA raises their fees. That's why you want to do your research before you purchase. Read the meeting minutes to find out about future HOA fee increases, so you are prepared.

Appreciation and Depreciation

Remember that your property value may appreciate (go up in value) or depreciate (go down in value) over time. This is called the market "ebb and flow" and it really should not affect you. Your home is your family's sanctuary and it's worth much more than just a dollar value on paper.

If your house value decreases, it won't affect you. Because you have a low-payment fixed-rate mortgage, you can still afford to pay it every month.

If the house appreciates in value, you aren't going to get another loan against it, so it won't matter right now. But the increased equity will be helpful when you move up to a larger home; and over time, your house will probably continue to increase in value.

8. Review Your Budget

You worked so hard to get your budget into tip-top shape, so now continue the great financial habits that you have developed. Keep up the good work by tracking your income and expenses and keeping a careful eye on your money. Continue reviewing your budget and challenging yourself and your family to do better each month.

Keep Track of your Income and Expenses

A budget spreadsheet is included in the Appendix and on the website. In our budget, we grouped the expenses into the following categories so it is easy to spot trends in your spending. Below are the major categories we use for our budget. The goal is to put more into the "savings" and "debt payoff" categories, while putting less into the "miscellaneous" and "other" categories. The categories are:

- Housing
- Automobiles
- Health/medical
- Utilities
- Food
- Education/child care
- Savings
- Debt payoff
- Miscellaneous
- Other

For example, if you have 2 cars, you can see that by eliminating 1 car, you can cut out many expenses, including the car payment, gasoline, maintenance, and government fees.

In the blank budget form, enter your projected monthly expenses at the beginning of the year. Then, after each month is over, put in your actual expenses, and see how it compares to your projection. Remember that your budget should be flexible, as your family needs will change. The budget is merely a tool to gauge your financial health.

Our sample is included as a PDF file, but we can download the Excel file from our web site, *www.HouseProAcademy.com*, where you can also find some useful budget forms.

Review your Budget Together as a Family Every Month

Keep the whole family involved by showing your children the basic budget. You can get them to stay committed by setting rewards as you reach various goals. More than money, children want your time and attention. For example, a day playing at the local park and then stopping to get ice cream on the way home could be more meaningful than going to an expensive theme park.

We have a blank budget and a sample budget in our appendix at the end of this book. They are also online on our web site. Try this online budget help from Dave Ramsey, host of his popular financial advice show: *www.MyTotalMoneyMakeover.com*

Your Children Learn the Right Way to Handle Money

If you start now, and train your children the right way when they are young, you will be so happy when they are older and have learned to be self-sufficient. Are your values, such as hard work, incorporated into your family? Children need to learn that money comes with effort, and they have to earn it by working. By showing them your example of hard work and good money management, they too can become homeowners.

When I was a little girl, our daddy had a huge 10-gallon water bottle and he would empty his spare change into it every day. It was such a huge bottle and seemed like it took forever to fill up. We would do odd jobs to earn money and put our quarters, dimes, and nickels in the bottle, too.

When it was full, that is when we really got excited! We got to dump out the bottle on the living room carpet, count up all the money, and spend it on a fun family activity that we selected.

One time, we had enough money for dinner at the local pizza parlor and we played Pac-Man video games all night. Another time, we chose to go to a local amusement park and play mini-golf.

Looking back, I think the best part was watching our money grow in the bottle. It is a great visual lesson for children to teach the value of saving money.

Your Home is Not an ATM

Remember that your home is also an asset. It's real property which can appreciate (go up in value) and also depreciate (go down in value).

However, you should not view your home as an investment. In other words, if the value increases, do not, and I repeat DO NOT, refinance or get a Home Equity Line of Credit (HELOC) loan to tap into the equity and pull out money. Refinance only to get a lower interest rate and do not take out cash.

The housing crisis that began in 2006 was caused, in part, by the rapid appreciation of real estate, and homeowners pulling out their new-found equity. Granted, some used the funds to pay off consumer debts, medical bills, legal fees, home improvements, and college education, which are worthy objectives, but other homeowners used the funds for travel and trips, luxury car purchases, and other items that were beyond their budget. The point is that you will need to live within your current income, and not depend upon the equity in your home when values appreciate.

On the other hand, if your house depreciates, you shouldn't be overly concerned, as long as you still have adequate income and you can afford the monthly mortgage payments. Remember, the purpose of your home is a safe, secure place for your family to flourish... not a monetary investment.

9. Protect Your Assets

Today, we will touch briefly on some basics of asset protection. As you learn more over the years and grow your portfolio, you will want to pursue more advanced asset protection strategies. Now that you're a homeowner, how can you protect your largest investment, your home?

- Get life insurance
- Meet with a financial planner
- Hire an attorney to create a living trust

Keep Everything you Worked so Hard to Acquire

When we get up and go to work every day, we do it with joy in our step and a gleam in our eye because we know WHAT we are working towards. We are doing it for our family and for our future. Throughout our lifetime, we work hard to reach our life goals such as buying a home, sending our children to college, and retiring with a nest egg to enjoy life.

> *"If you die without a Will, then the state automatically provides one for you; it is much more complex for your survivors, and the distribution of your assets may not be as you desired." p.340 (Abts, 2002)*

You have heard the saying, *"It takes a team to realize the dream!"* It's so true. We recommend that you hire a team of top professionals to help you reach your goals. You can achieve so much more with your team behind you.

Life Insurance is Important

Life insurance is valuable because it will help to replace your income and your earning power, should you become permanently disabled or pass away unexpectedly. It will allow your family to continue paying the mortgage and stay on track toward good financial stewardship. In the event that you are no longer alive, or if you are not able to work due to a massive injury, the life insurance policy will pay a cash settlement to your heirs.

The most important thing you need to know is that there are 2 basic types of life insurance: whole and term. A great insurance agent can help you determine which plan is right for you and your family. If your current insurance agent also sells life insurance, that is great. Be sure to contact her or him. If not, your financial advisor can help you select an agent that has a track record of success with families like yours.

Get Solid Advice from a Financial Advisor

A great financial advisor can help you look at your overall budget and recommend strategies to help you increase your income, protect your assets, and plan for the future. Some financial planners also advise you regarding life insurance, estate planning, and investing in securities. Look for a professional whom you can trust. Check out our web site for tips on how to interview and find a great financial advisor.

The main tip I would give you for hiring a financial planner would be to select a professional with a CFP designation (certified financial planner), or possibly even a chartered financial counselor (ChFC) or Personal Financial Specialist. You can find a local CFP in your area by searching that website.

You should know that there are 2 types of financial planners: fee-based (they charge you a flat fee for a consultation) or commission-based (they earn money by selling you stocks and other products). For the basic starting needs of a first-time homebuyer, I would recommend starting with a fee-only planner. To locate fee-only advisors in your area, check the National Association of Personal Financial Advisors at *www.napfa.org* or Garrett Planning Network at *http://garrettplanning.com*.

Create a Living Trust for your Family

Yes, now that you own a major asset, you need a "Will". Your attorney can help you prepare one right away. Do you have a legal service plan? For example, if you are a LegalShield® member and have a LegalShield® family plan, a "Will" is included at no additional cost. Remember to update it every year.

Many estate plans contain the following 4 critical elements, which your attorney can advise and explain in detail:

- Last Will and testament
- Family living trust
- Advance health care directive
- Durable power of attorney

Many families use living trusts and land trusts (title-holding trusts) to secure their assets from creditors, predators, and unnecessary taxes. A land trust, also known as a title-holding trust, is a more sophisticated strategy that is beyond the scope of this guide.

> *"The concept of the living trust is to provide you and your heirs with continuity in the ownership and management of your property, along with the traditional estate tax deferrals and avoidances. If it is important to you that your property is transferred to your heirs without the interruption and involvement of third parties and the unnecessary costs incident thereto, the living trust is for you." (Platt, 2012)*

Today our advice is to make an appointment with your attorney to discuss a family living trust. Holding your property in a living trust is superior to holding property in your name, for many reasons. The primary benefit of a living trust is the continuance of your estate. If your living trust is designed and funded correctly, upon you or your spouse's death, your property will go to whom you want, when you want, without going through the court system. Most importantly, your estate will not have to go through probate court.

Your attorney may advise you to avoid probate court because it is quite expensive, it will take years to settle your estate, and your wishes may not be followed, (with regard to the inheritance of your property and assets). With your living trust, the transfer of your property will happen seamlessly and instantly, and best of all, your inheritance will not be available for the public to scrutinize through the court records. It also offers some privacy and; therefore, may protect you from frivolous and predatory lawsuits.

> *"I have seen the emotional and financial stress and uncertainty experienced by families when they are faced with the probate of a loved one's estate. After the death of a loved one, the family should spend time healing and adjusting to the loss of their loved one, not meeting with attorneys and attending court hearings. A living trust can ease this concern." (Rolcik, 2007)*

Depending on the property tax laws in your state, property placed in your living trust may avoid probate taxes for your heirs and may save money on property tax transfer fees due to "step-up value" tax laws.

Hire an Attorney to Help You

As a consumer, you may need different types of legal assistance. Attorneys specialize in different areas of law, so when you are ready to prepare your living trust, you will need to contact an attorney who is experienced in estate planning. I suggest that you get your living trust prepared as soon as you purchase your home. Ask your friends for a referral and find a great estate-planning attorney in your area.

> *"If you have seen a Living Trust before, you have found that they are somewhat lengthy. In my office, the typical Living Trust is 50 pages long." p.6 (Condon, 2008)*

Sometimes homeowners are reluctant to contact an attorney, because they believe the fees will be too high. It is true that hourly attorney fees can be quite expensive. Did you know that there are alternatives to paying hourly fees? One legal service that we have had great success with is LegalShield®, (formerly known as Pre-Paid Legal). LegalShield® offers members a nationwide network of provider law firms that are carefully screened, selected, and monitored for quality. Many services are included with the membership, and additional services are offered at a discount. Go to ***www.LegalShield.com*** or ***www.BrownBiz.net***, which is my site.

As LegalShield® members, we simply pay a small monthly fee and in return, we are able to receive many benefits that would normally be out of the reach of the average consumer or small business owner. We have saved thousands of dollars by having all of our documents reviewed, letters written, and questions answered by high quality attorneys.

We only pay $20 per month for a family plan or $50 for a family PLUS small business plan. We feel it is one of the best ways we protect our family. If you are interested in finding out more, visit our website at www.BrownBiz.net or contact a LegalShield® rep in your local area.

Leave a Legacy for your Family

Another reason to get a great attorney and a financial advisor on your team is to help you strategize the best way to pass on your property to your heirs, while owing the least amount of inheritance and taxes.

After all, you worked hard and saved your money so you could leave an inheritance for your children and grandchildren to enjoy. You did not work hard to leave an inheritance that costs your heirs taxes and attorney fees and leaves them with nothing.

> *"We are convinced that real estate continues to be one of the most appealing ways for you to achieve financial security, and, along the way, to enjoy — indeed love — your investment in ways that you could never love stocks, bonds, and bank accounts." p.189 (Smith, 2008)*

We, as parents and grandparents, are willing to sacrifice so that our children and grandchildren have better opportunities in the future. Leaving a home for our children to own is a wonderful legacy. Not every family will be in a situation to do so, but we applaud those who can.

CONCLUSION

Well, we are nearing the end of our book for first-time homebuyers. By now, I'm sure your head is spinning with great information. You learned about the 9 steps to follow to buy your first home and become a home owner. So what is next? Let's keep the momentum going by taking action today.

Prepare Now

Start planning for your family long-term. Think about where your family is going to live in the future, and think about their security. Your vision is to leave a good financial legacy for your children. It all starts now, today, this moment.

Remember, Home Buying is a Process

If there was anything that will stick in our mind about this guide, it should be that home buying is a PROCESS. We now know that there are steps we have to do, one step at a time, to reach our destination. We don't expect anything to be instant, but we are following the procedures and we will be prepared to act quickly when needed.

Do the Footwork Yourself

We learned about what to do in preparing to purchase a home, and we learned what not to do. We found out that our goal is achievable if we simply follow the steps. We also found out that we need to save our money and learn to be good stewards over our finances. We know that it is important to handle our credit well. While we need to establish good credit, we should not incur or charge any more credit accounts. In fact, while we are going through the loan process, we should not change jobs or bank accounts, either.

We found out that we are going to have to do some homework ourselves. We will have to track and manage our budget, check our credit score and work to improve it, and gather documents for the mortgage lender. We will need to drive around neighborhoods, preview the exterior of homes, and research communities to find out where we want to live. We have to sign a lot of documents and attend a home inspection and read reports and then sign more documents!

Your REALTOR® Negotiates for You

In this book, we learned the value of hiring a great REALTOR® to guide you through the process. Our REALTOR® will show us homes, negotiate with the seller's agent, and write up our purchase offer. You and your family will be very involved in the entire home buying process, but your trusted REALTOR® will guide you through from start to finish. You can depend on professionals who have years of experience in helping first-time homebuyers.

YOU Can Be a Homeowner

In this guide, you heard success stories of various homebuyers like you. You received many tips and tools that you will use. You took great notes and you are totally prepared. Now you know that your dream of home ownership can become a reality. At this point, you are not certain how long the process is going to take. However long it takes, you are committed to your goal and you will become a homeowner soon.

Take Action Today

The most important thing you can do is to start by taking action now. It is great to have the education, but education does not mean anything unless you put it to use. Your goal, your dream of home ownership may seem insurmountable.

If you are worried that the process is complex, or anxious that you may not qualify, there is only one solution: Take a step of faith. Start today, right now, and make a promise to yourself and your family that, going forward, every single day you will take a step towards your dream and before you know it, your dream of home ownership will become reality.

Questions?

Do you have any questions about our guidebook? If so, please contact us. We would love to hear from you! We especially enjoy hearing about your first home buying experience and what you learned in the process.

Forms and Samples

In the Appendix are included samples of the following documents.

1. Wish List

2. Budget Sample & Blank Form
3. Loan Comparison Form
4. Rent vs. Own Calculation
5. Agent Interview
6. House Comparison Form
7. Vendors on Your Team
8. Offer Checklist

Check our web site for samples of the following forms:

1. Rent vs. Own Comparison
2. Mortgage Payments
3. Budget Worksheet
4. Credit Report
5. Pre-Qualification Letter
6. 1003 Mortgage Loan Application
7. Home Comparison Form
8. Purchase Offer/Contract
9. Escrow Process Flowchart
10. Title Vesting Chart
11. Pest Control Report
12. Home Building Inspection
13. Appraisal
14. Title Report
15. Home Warranty
16. Statement of Identity
17. HUD-1 Closing Statement
18. Escrow company Closing Statement
19. Sample Budget

As a disclosure, some sample forms are from actual transactions. You can still get a good idea of what your documents will look like by viewing these sample forms. We have crossed out any sensitive information on the forms.

Resources

Check out our web site for resources available at your fingertips. Download free forms, view sample documents, and click links to resourceful information at *www.HouseProAcademy.com*.

Watch for our upcoming courses such as:

- Home Ownership Maintenance
- Green Home and Energy Efficiency
- Home Health and Safety

Action Steps

So now, you know you are going to become a homeowner soon. What are the action steps to take?

1. Have a family meeting
2. Make list of house "needs and wants"
3. Hire a top Realtor®
4. Review your credit report
5. Meet with a mortgage lender
6. Start shopping for homes

Now you have finished this guide, and you are ready to take action. The first thing you are going to do is call a family meeting. This is a very important meeting because you want everybody's support. Gather your household together and share your goals, your dreams, and your vision. Explain the benefits and ask for their commitment to work together to reach your goals. Let your family know how important it is for you all to be in agreement and commit to buying a home together.

Tell your family about this guide and attend a home buying workshop with them. Take the time to ask each person what he or she would like to have in the new home. Make a list of everyone's needs and wants. Remember to caution everyone that although you have a wish list, no house will perfectly meet all of your needs and wants. It is okay to start with a big wish list because you all have big hopes, goals, and dreams.

Next on our list is to interview and hire a top Realtor® who can guide us along the path to home ownership and help make our dreams come true. A great REALTOR® is a licensed real estate agent who is a member of the National Association of REALTORS®, the state association of REALTORS®, and the local association of REALTORS®. This professional is knowledgeable and experienced in helping search for your first home, and will uphold high standards of excellence.

You are going to need a great mortgage lender. Remember our formula: Research 5, interview 3, and select 1. This person is the professional who will help you qualify for financing that's affordable and fits in your budget.

Before you meet with your mortgage lender, you are going to review your credit report and check it for errors. You want to make sure that there are not any mistakes on your credit before the lender runs your report.

Now you're ready! Let's get going.

APPENDIX

- Glossary
- Acronyms
- Bibliography
- Index

Glossary

Terms & Definitions

NOTE: Terms are explained in simple, easy-to-understand words. These are not legal definitions. They are the author's opinion based on her knowledge, experience, and research.

100% Financing

A mortgage loan that does not require a down payment from the payment (does not mean that closing costs are waived or paid).

1031 Exchange

A technique of selling one property without having to pay current capital gains taxes because the seller is simultaneously acquiring another property.

Additional Principal Payments

Additional money that a homeowner (borrower) pays to reduce their mortgage balance due.

Amenities

Valuable items included in a house purchase, and could be part of the community also, such as an HOA swimming pool.

American Dream

The admired ideals of freedom as embodied by the culture of the United States of America.

Appliances

Large electronic items often included with sale of a house. For example: stove/oven/range, dishwasher, refrigerator, clothes washer and dryer, micro-hood.

Appraisal

A written report by a licensed appraiser, including an opinion of a house's value.

Appreciation

The amount of value that a property has increased.

Approval Letter

Letter from a mortgage lender that includes a commitment to loan you an exact amount of money, on a specific house, with a specific closing date. It states the interest rate and payment amounts.

Approved

Buyer who has received an approval letter from his/her mortgage lender.

Assets

Items of value that you own.

Attorney Closing

An escrow/settlement process in a state that utilizes attorneys instead of escrow companies. States that requires an attorney for deed preparation include FL, GA, IL, KY, LA, MD, MA, MI, NJ, NY, NC, OH, OR, SC, TX, VA, WA, DC, WV.

Back End Ratio

Your "front end" housing payment PLUS all your monthly consumer debts.

Backup Offer / Backup Position

An offer that is submitted to a seller already under contract, just in case the current buyer backs up.

Backup Plan (AKA **Plan B**)

An alternative strategy that you will take, if your 1st strategy doesn't work out.

Bidding Process

Home buyers who are all competing for the same house at the same time.

Budget

A spreadsheet that calculates a family's income, expenses, & savings.

Buyer Representation Agreement (BRA or BRE)

A contract to hire a buyer's agent. Sometimes called a **Buyer Broker Agreement**.

Cash Reserves

Money in an account which can be liquefied (withdrawn) if needed.

Certified Funds

A money order or a cashier's check issued by a credible bank.

Closing Attorney

Closing attorneys are required to direct the closing process in some states. States that requires an attorney for deed preparation include FL, GA, IL, KY, LA, MD, MA, MI, NJ, NY, NC, OH, OR, SC, TX, VA, WA, DC, WV.

Closing Costs

The fees charged to buyers and sellers that are paid as part of the cost of the transaction.

Closing Period (AKA **Escrow Period** Or **Settlement Period**)

The time frame of the transaction purchase finalizing.

Community Property

Property that is owned jointly by husband and wife, even if both of their names are not on the legal title.

Competitive Offer

Purchase offer which has a high price and good terms, backed by a solid, qualified buyer.

Comps / Comparables

Houses that are in a similar neighborhood, and are similar sizes, and were built around the same time period, are called "comparable" because they can be compared to each other.

Concessions

Credits or favorable monetary terms extended from the seller to the buyer.

Condo / Condominium

A housing project with attached walls, where each homeowner owns their own unit.

Consumer Debt

Any credit account you used to buy electronic goods, household furniture, take vacations, buy clothing and jewelry, and spend for Christmas presents or anything that is not considered an appreciating asset.

Consummated

Officially started or began something, such as a contract going into effect.

Contingency (AKA **Subject To**)

Certain conditions that must be fulfilled in order for the purchase to proceed.

Contingency Period

The time frame in which conditions are fulfilled before the purchase contract is in full effect and can proceed.

Conventional Loan

A mortgage loan that is NOT issued or insured by a government agency, such as Fannie Mae or HUD.

Convey

Items that will be staying with the property upon sale because they are included with the purchase of the house.

Co-Payment

A small, flat fee that a homeowner pays in lieu of the entire cost of a repair. With a home warranty.

Co-Sign

When a buyer/borrower is not strongly qualified, a co-signer is an additional person who signs on the loan as a guarantor.

Counter Offer

An acceptance of an offer, but with some changes.

Credit Bureau

1 of the 3 major companies that sells credit reports & credit scores.

Credit Counselor

A professional who assists consumers to lower their debt by paying off credit accounts and challenging inaccurate credit entries.

Credit Scores

FICO scores from 3 consumer credit reports, rating each consumer's credit-worthiness and the likelihood they will repay their debts on time.

Crime Statistics

Calculations about various types of crimes in a neighborhood or city.

Customary Split

The responsibility for paying standard fees, which are typical for your region.

Debt Consolidation

The process of taking several debts and combining them all into 1 single, smaller payment.

Debt Ratio

These debts are measured against your monthly income and calculated as a ratio.

Debt-Free

A lifestyle choice of living without owning anyone any money.

Decision-Makers

People who have a vested interest in a transaction and the ability to influence the parties (buyers & sellers).

Deductible

When an insurance claim is filed, the deductible is the amount of money that the policy holder must pay before insurance begins paying its share.

Delayed Gratification

The concept of waiting until later to purchase things.

Demographic Data

Info by zip codes, such as the average income of a household, the educational level, and number of people in a family.

Depreciation

The amount of value that a property has decreased.

Disclosures

Documents that communicate important info from one party to another or document the condition of the house. Some are required as legal disclaimers.

Disposable Income

The "extra" cash that is left over from your paycheck after you have paid all your necessary bills.

Downpayment (AKA "Down Payment")

The total amount of cash that home buyer is putting down (not including closing costs) usually expressed as a certain % of the purchase price.

Due Diligence

The process of investigating all of the features about a house to verify its condition. It is the buyers' responsibility to do their "due diligence" research before purchasing.

Earnest Money Deposit (EMD)

The check that the buyer writes as the initial down payment and submits with their purchase offer.

Electronic Signature (AKA e-Signature)

A digital signature applied to disc online or via a tech gadget.

Equity

The amount of ownership that you have in your house, over and above the amount you owe on the mortgage loan.

Escrow

The process of administering a real estate sales transaction. A neutral party to facilitate the money and the transaction between buyer and seller.

Escrow Company (AKA Settlement Company, depending on what state you're in)

The entity that holds the buyer's earnest money deposit while processing the transaction sale. In some areas, the title company also acts as the escrow company.

Escrow Officer (AKA Settlement Officer, depending on what state you're in)

An escrow company employee who is responsible for closing a transaction.

Escrow Funds (AKA Reserve Funds)

Money that the mortgage lender collects in addition to the mortgage payment. The additional funds are put into an **impound account** (AKA **escrow account**) and used to pay the borrower's property taxes and homeowners insurance.

Established Neighborhood

A community that is more mature because it's been in existence for many years.

Estimated Closing Statement (AKA Settlement Statement)

The HUD-1 or the escrow company calculation that shows a breakdown of buyer/seller credits and debits for closing.

FICO Score

Refer to **"credit scores"**.

Financial Habits

Putting into place a continuous system of good money management.

Financial Planner

A licensed professional who can assist you in reaching your family's goals. A certified or licensed business professional that helps families manages their finances wisely, grow wealth, and protect assets.

Floor Plan

Diagram of a house's layout, including a sketch of the rooms.

Free & Clear

Owning a home with no mortgage or liens against it.

Front End Ratio

Your total housing payment, including mortgage, PMI, property taxes, & insurance.

Good Money Management

The practice of accounting for income and expenses and overseeing it well.

Home Inspection (AKA **Structural Building Inspection**)

A structural inspection of the house by an experienced professional. The inspector will write a report stating the results of the inspection.

Home Warranty

A prepaid annual policy that guarantees broken items in the house will be fixed with only a small co-payment. The home warranty company will fix things when they break, with only a small co-payment due from the home owner. Similar to an insurance policy.

Homeowner

A person who owns the house they live in, with his/her name legally on title.

HomeOwner Association (HOA)

The association that makes rules for a neighborhood, collects monthly fees, and pays common-area expenses. HOA fees are mandatory if the home is in an HOA area.

Homeowners Insurance (AKA **Fire Insurance** Or **Hazard Insurance**)

Insurance that protects the house by guaranteeing the homeowners will be compensated in case of a loss. The insurance company pays for broken/burned real property which was covered in the policy.

Impound Account

Along with your mortgage payment each month, you pay additional money ("Escrow Reserves") to cover the cost of the property taxes and homeowners insurance. The mortgage company puts this money into an impound account, and then pays the insurance and taxes every year so the homeowner doesn't have to worry about paying it annually as a lump sum.

Instant Email Alerts

Newly listed houses for sale that are sent to home buyers.

Insurance Policy

A contract between a home owner and the insurance company that determines the claims which the company will cover.

Itemized Deductions

Expenses and credits that can be subtracted from the tax payer's 1040 tax return. Compare to standard deductions.

Legacy

Something that you create, either tangible or intangible, from which future generations will benefit.

Legal Obligation

Something you are committed to do because it is a law or because you have signed a written, legally binding contract.

Legal Service Plan

A membership-based business service that offers legal advice from attorneys to members at a low monthly cost. An example is LegalShield®.

Life Insurance

A written insurance policy that pays money to your dependents upon your death or permanent disability.

Life Span

The number of years an appliance (or home improvement) will typically last.

List Price (AKA Asking Price)

The amount of a seller markets his house that (not the same as value).

Living Trust (AKA Family Living Trust)

A legal entity formed for the purpose of protecting assets, such as real property.

Mello-Roos Fees

A common assessment (fee) in California which is billed to home owners.

Mortgage Insurance (AKA "PMI")

Mortgage insurance is required by mortgage lenders when you don't have a large enough downpayment (typically less than 20%). It protects the lender by covering losses they may incur if you default on your loan.

Mortgage Loan

A loan for debt that is secured against the house.

Move-Up Home

A house purchased by existing homeowners who are moving up to a bigger or better home. Compare to "Starter Home".

Mutual Agreement Of Both Parties

The seller and buyer have both agreed upon the price and terms.

Negotiable

An item that is subject to discussion between the parties.

Negotiation Process

When the buyer and seller are discussing what each party will give and take.

Neighborhood Blight

Conditions that de-value a community.

Nest Egg

Money that is put aside for retirement and future planning.

Notary Public

A person commission by the State who is present to notarize your signature on legal documents, such as the mortgage loan documents.

Offer / Purchase Offer / Offer to Purchase (AKA Bid)

A document from a buyer to a seller to purchase.

Open Escrow

Process of a neutral party (escrow company) starting to process a sale transaction after all parties have executed (signed) the contract.

Overlap Occupancy

Having possession of 2 houses to enable you to move out of 1 house and into another easily.

Owner-Occupant Buyers

Families who will live in the home they buy.

Personal Property

Items that are not real property and not included in the home purchase.

Pest Control Inspection (AKA **Termite Inspection**)

An inspection to check the building's structural integrity due to possible damage by termites (wood-destroying pests) or water. The report is divided into Sections 1 and 2. Most mortgage lenders will require a Certificate of Clearance for Section 1.

Planned Unit Development (PUD)

A housing project where each homeowner owns a part of the common areas and the entire community is governed by rules.

Preliminary Title Report (AKA "Prelim")

A search of the legal ownership of a house and any liens against it, or other challenges to the legal title.

Pre-Payment Penalty

A large lump sum of money that a borrower must pay to their mortgage lender in order to pay off their mortgage early.

Pre-Qualification Letter

Letter from a mortgage lender that includes the dollar amount for which you are qualified to show for houses. It's an unofficial estimate and is not highly regarded for accuracy.

Pre-Qualified

Buyer who has received a pre-qualification letter from his/her mortgage lender.

Preventive Maintenance

The process of keeping the house repaired and maintained on a regular basis to lessen the change of major repair crises.

Price Range

A dollar amount that varies from a low amount to high amount.

Principal

The amount of money borrowed on your mortgage loan that must be paid back.

Property Taxes

A real estate tax assessed & collected by the county, based on the value of the property.

Purchase Contract (AKA Sales Contract)

An agreement between a buyer and a seller of a house for sale.

Qualification Letter

Letter from a mortgage lender that includes desktop underwriting (DU) approval stating how much money you can borrow and the interest rate of the loan.

Qualified

Buyer who has received a qualification letter from his/her mortgage lender.

Ratified Contract (AKA Fully Executed)

Document signed by all parties to make it a legal agreement.

REALTOR®

A real estate agent who is a member of the National Association of Realtors®.

Recorded Deed

The Deed of Trust (AKA warranty deed) officially and legally transfer to new owner recorded at the county clerk- recorder's office, which now becomes a publicly recorded document.

REO (AKA Bank Owned)

House that is owned by the mortgage lender who foreclosed on the house.

Repair Request

The buyer can request that the seller to either: fix the broken items, give a repair credit, or lower the purchase price to compensate for the broken items.

Search Criteria

Items that buyers categorize to help them find houses that meet their families' needs, such as list price, zip codes, and number of bedrooms.

Seasoned Funds

Money that has been sitting in the buyer's bank account for a certain number of months (usually 2 months).

Service Call

The cost for a contractor to visit the house and inspect or fix repairs.

Settlement Company (AKA **Escrow Company, depending on what state you're in**)

The entity that holds the buyer's earnest money deposit while processing the transaction sale.

Settlement Officer (AKA **Escrow Officer, depending on what state you're in**)

A settlement company employee who is responsible for closing a transaction.

Short Sale

Sale of a house which has a higher mortgage than the value of the house, therefore the mortgage lender must approve the sale.

Sign Off On Contract (AKA **Remove All Contingencies**)

Buyer agrees to proceed with finalizing the purchase, and now cannot back out without a penalty.

Single Family Residence (AKA **"SFR"**)

A stick-built house that is detached (no common walls with other houses).

Special Assessments

Additional taxes or HOA fees, above the regular fees, charged to the property owner.

Standard Forms

Contract and disclosure templates that are used by many REALTORS®.

Starter Home

The first home that is purchased by home buyers, which may not be the best, the biggest, or their perfect dream home.

Structural Condition

The quality of the house frame, including foundation, floors, roof, and walls.

Subject To (AKA Contingent Upon)

Certain conditions that must be fulfilled in order for the purchase to proceed.

Table Funding

Where all parties gather around the closing table as the loan document signing, loan funding, and closing happens all at once. This is a typical closing procedure for certain states.

Tax Deductions

Expenses that can be deducted from your income tax bill.

Tax-Deductible

An expense or a credit that you can report on your annual tax return, in order to lower your taxes due.

Title Company

A company that guarantees ownership for the new buyer.

Title Insurance

A policy in which the ownership of the property has been researched and the company will guarantee the buyers that they are getting a legitimate ownership.

Title Vesting / Vesting Of Title

The legal ownership of the house and how that ownership is held.

Twin Home

A semi-detached house that shares 1 common wall with another house. Each house is separately owned by different owners.

Under Contract

Both buyer and seller have signed a purchase contract and come to a mutual agreement on price terms. They are locked into an agreement so the house is considered to be NOT available for purchase to any other buyers.

Underwriting / Loan Underwriting

Mortgage lender's department that will approve your loan. They must examine all of your documents and you must meet their strict criteria.

Value / Valuation

How much a house is worth (NOT the same as **Asking Price** or **List Price**)

Values

Ideals incorporated into your family, such as hard work, being debt-free, contributing to charities, generous giving, faith in God, saving money, and community participation.

Walk-Through Inspection (AKA Verification Of Property Condition)

When the buyers do their final walk-through before closing, they sign a form to verify its condition.

Will

A legal written directive that outlines your wishes to your heirs and the court. It specifies what actions are to happen to your property after you die.

Wire

Funds that are transferred to a bank account electronically.

Wish List

A buyer's list of features and requirements for a house purchase.

Zero-Down Loan

A loan that does not require a down payment from the buyer.

Acronyms

1003	Loan application form from Freddie Mac
ABR	Accredited Buyer's Representative (designation from National Association of REALTORS®)
APN	Assessor's Parcel Number (tax ID number)
ASHI	American Society of Home Inspectors
AVID	Agent Visual Inspection Disclosure form (form from California Association of REALTORS®)
BPI	Building Performance Institute is a certification for energy auditors and home performance contractors who inspect homes for energy efficiency and report on the measurements found in an Energy Audit Report.
CC&R	Covenants, Codes, and Restrictions
CFP	Certified Financial Planner (designation)
ChFC	Chartered Financial Counselor (designation)
CID	Common Interest Development
CMA	Comparable Market Analysis
COE	Close of Escrow
CREIA	California Real Estate Inspection Association
DU	Desktop Underwriting (loan approval)
EMD	Earnest Money Deposit check
FHA	Federal Housing Administration (government agency that underwrites/guarantees mortgage loans)
FSBO	For Sale By Owner (house for sale)
GFE	Good Faith Estimate (mortgage loan form)
GRI	Graduate REALTOR® Institute (designation from National Association of REALTORS®)
HERS	Home Energy Rating System (HERS) Index, the nationally recognized scoring system for measuring a home's energy performance and rating a home's energy efficiency.
HOA	Home Owners Association

HUD	U.S. Department of Housing and Urban Development (government agency)
HUD-1	Standard real estate settlement form for federally regulated mortgage loans
InterNACHI	International Association of Certified Home Inspectors
LOE	Letter Of Explanation (mortgage loan form)
MLS	Multiple Listing Service
NACA	Neighborhood Assistance Corporation of America (non-profit organization)
NAHI	National Association of Home Inspectors
NSF	Not Sufficient Funds (returned/bounced check)
P&L	Profit and Loss (financial statement for business owners)
PITI	Principal, Interest, Taxes, And Insurance
PMI	Private Mortgage Insurance
POC	Paid Outside of Closing (expenses not paid through the escrow process)
POF	Proof of Funds
PUD	Planned Unit Development
REO	Real Estate Owned (bank owned property)
RPA-CA	Residential Purchase Agreement and Joint Escrow Instructions (form from California Association of REALTORS®)
SFR	Single Family Residence
SI	Statement of Identity form (AKA Statement of Information) from title company
USDA	U.S. Department of Agriculture (government agency that administers mortgage loans)
VA	U.S. Department of Veterans Affairs (government agency that underwrites/guarantees mortgage loans)
VOE	Verification Of Employment (mortgage loan form)
VOF	Verification Of Funds (mortgage loan form)
VOI	Verification Of Income (mortgage loan form)
VOR	Verification Of Rent Paid (mortgage loan form)

VP   Verification of Property Condition (form from California Association of
                REALTORS®)

Bibliography

Abts, H. (2002). *The Living Trust: The Failproof Way to Pass Along your Estate to Your Heirs.* New York: McGraw-Hill.

Becker, N. (2011). *The Complete Book of Home Inspection.* New York: McGraw-Hill.

Bray, I. &. (2011). *Nolo's Essential Guide to Buying Your First Home.* Berkeley, CA: Nolo.

Buffini, B. (2008). *Getting Buyers Off the Fence*, blog. Retrieved from Buffini & Company: http://www.buffiniandcompany.com/Blog/post/2008/03/Getting-Buyers-Off-the-Fence.aspx

Charloff, J. (2011). *Practical Guide to Home Inspection: What you need to know before you buy a home.* Los Angeles: Sweet Rain Press.

Cohen, H. (1982). *You Can Negotiate Anything: The World's Best Negotiator Tells You How To Get What You Want.* New York: McGraw-Hill.

Condon, J. (2008). *The Living Trust Advisor: Everything You Need to Know About Your Living Trust.* Hoboken, NJ: John Wiley & Sons, Inc.

Conner, N. (2010). *Buying a Home: The Missing Manual.* Sebastopol, CA: O'Reilly Media, Inc.

Diamond, S. (2010). *Getting More: How You Can Negotiate to Succeed in Work and Life.* New York: Three Rivers Press.

Gadow, S. (2003). *The Complete Guide to Your Real Estate Closing: Answers to All Your Questions -- from Opening Escrow, to Negotiating Fees, to Signing the Closing Papers.* New York: McGraw-Hill.

Glink, I. (2000). *100 Questions Every First-Time Home Buyer Should Ask: With Answers from Top Brokers from Around the Country.* New York: Three Rivers Press.

Holmes, M. (2012). *The Holmes Inspection.* Des Moines, IA: Time Home Entertainment Inc. Books.

Irwin, R. (2002). *How to Buy a Home When You Can't Afford It.* New York: McGraw-Hill.

Kavoussi, B. (2012, 03 22). *Buying A Home Cheaper Than Renting In 98 Percent Of Housing Markets.* Retrieved from The Huffington Post: http://www.huffingtonpost.com/2012/03/22/buying-a-home-cheaper-than-renting_n_1372855.html

Levinrad, L. &. (2009). Title Insurance Tips and Secrets. (Kindle e-Book). Boca Raton, FL: Distressed Real Estate Institute, Inc.

Moy, D. (2003). *Living Trusts, 3rd Edition.* Hoboken, NJ: John Wiley & Sons, Inc.

National Association of Realtors. (2012). *Report: Social Benefits of Homeownership and Stable Housing.* Retrieved from http://www.realtor.org/reports/social-benefits-of-homeownership-and-stable-housing

National Association of Realtors®. (2012). *Profile of Home Buyers and Sellers 2011.* Washington DC : National Association of Realtors®.

Nielsen, G. (2009, November 28). *Personal Finance.* Retrieved from Investopedia: http://www.investopedia.com/articles/mortgages-real-estate/08/home-ownership.asp#axzz2BqRSvqHn

Peebles, N. (2012). Should I Buy A Home: Rent vs Buy. Kindle e-Book.

Perkins, B. (2002, December 19). California's Controversial New Construction Defect Law. California, U.S.: RealtyTimes. Retrieved from http://realtytimes.com/rtpages/20021219_defectlaw.htm

Platt, H. (2012). Your Living Trust and Estate Plan: How to Maximize Your Family's Assets and Protect Your Loved Ones. (Kindle e-Book). New York: Allworth Press.

Reed, D. (2008). *Mortgages 101: Quick Answers to Over 250 Critical Questions About Your Home Loan.* New York: Amacom.

Rolcik, K. (2007). *The Complete Living Trust Kit: An Essential Guide to Control Your Estate and Easily Pass It to Your Family* (Kindle e-Book ed.). Naperville, IL: Sphinx Publishing.

Rowley, L. &. (2007). *Cheap Insurance for Your Home, Automobile, Health, & Life: How to Save Thousands While Getting Good Coverage.* Ocala, FL: Atlantic Publishing Group, Inc.

Smith, G. &. (2008). *Houseonomics: Why Owning a Home is Still a Great Investment.* Upper Saddle River, NJ: FT Press.

Tara-Nicholle Nelson, E. (2006). *The Savvy Woman's Homebuying Handbook.* Oakland, CA: Prosperity Way Enterprises LLC.

The Augusta Chronicle. (2002, 12 23). Discrepancies in credit reports can be harmful. *Associated Press.* Retrieved from http://chronicle.augusta.com/stories/2002/12/23/bus_365469.shtml

Thomas, J. (2005). *Negotiate to Win: The 21 Rules for Successful Negotiating.* New York: HarperCollins Publishers.

Weston, L. (2012). *Your Credit Score: How to Improve the 3-Digit Number that Shapes your Financial Future.* Upper Saddle River, NJ: FT Press.

Index

100% 26, 32, 41, 59, 60, 76, 78, 82, 163
1003 .... 55, 159, 177
1031 163
ABR 28, 177
Additional Principal Payments 38, 163
Amenities 48, 50, 90, 163
American Dream .... i, 83, 163
Apartment 65
APN 100, 177
Appliances 16, 17, 46, 79, 83, 86, 87, 96, 101, 133, 134, 146, 163
Appraisal 41, 101, 103, 122, 159, 163
Appreciate 24, 149
Appreciation.. 15, 149, 163
Approval Letter 58, 128, 163, 164
Approved..164
ASHI...93, 177
Assets.. 18, 45, 55, 127, 152, 153, 164, 169, 171
Attorney Closing 164
AVID.. 135, 177
Back End Ratio 164
Backup Offer 164
Backup Plan 107, 108, 111, 115, 116, 164
Bidding Process 164
BPI 74, 177
Budget.. 15, 16, 31, 33, 34, 35, 41, 42, 46, 48, 57, 78, 82, 110, 112, 126, 147, 150, 152, 158, 159, 160, 164
Buyer Representation Agreement 164
Cash Reserves 42, 164
CC&R 63, 67, 124, 125, 177
Certified Funds... 118, 138, 164
CFP... 153, 177
ChFC 153, 177
CID 63, 177
Closing Attorney 164
Closing Costs ..26, 32, 41, 51, 52, 76, 91, 92, 97, 99, 101, 103, 105, 106, 108, 131, 133, 135, 137, 163, 165, 167
Closing Period 87, 165
CMA 87, 90, 177
COE 177
Community Property 165
Competitive Offer 165
Comps 85, 87, 89, 90, 91, 122, 165
Concessions...165
Condominium.. 56, 63, 165
Condos..64
Consumer Debt... 31, 33, 34, 38, 39, 41, 164, 165
Consummated 165

Contingency 165
Contingency Period.. 165
Conventional Loan... 166
Convey 166
Co-Payment 96, 147, 148, 166, 169
Co-Sign 166
Counter Offer 90, 100, 107, 108, 109, 110, 111, 166
Credit Bureau 36, 55, 166
Credit Counselor 37, 166
Credit Scores 166, 168
CREIA... 93, 177
Crime Statistics 49, 166
Customary Split 92, 106, 166
Debt Consolidation 32, 166
Debt Ratio 34, 40, 58, 126, 133, 167
Debt-Free.. 32, 33, 34, 167, 176
Decision-Makers... 47, 48, 60, 167
Deductible... 167
Delayed Gratification 34, 167
Demographic Data 49, 167
Depreciate... 63, 149
Depreciation 24, 149, 167
Detached Home... 62
Disclosures................................ 17, 97, 99, 102, 117, 118, 123, 124, 167
Disposable Income.. 33, 167
Downpayment26, 27, 28, 41, 44, 51, 52, 54, 56, 57, 60, 76, 97, 100, 105, 133, 135, 138, 163,
     167, 168, 171, 176
DU 58, 128, 173, 177
Due Diligence 112, 167
Duplex... 65
Earnest Money Deposit........................ 41, 56, 60, 75, 76, 100, 118, 121, 127, 168, 174
Electronic Signature 97, 168
EMD 75, 97, 118, 177
Equity 16, 43, 83, 151, 168
Escrow ...17, 28, 41, 60, 72, 75, 76, 86, 87, 88, 89, 92, 95, 99, 102, 103, 104, 105, 114, 115,
     116, 117, 118, 119, 121, 124, 125, 127, 128, 129, 130, 131, 133, 135, 136, 137, 138, 139,
     142, 143, 147, 149, 159, 164, 165, 168, 172, 177, 178
Escrow Company...118
Escrow Officer 118, 128
Escrow Period 165
Established Neighborhood..168
Estimated Closing Statement 135, 168
FHA 41, 52, 64, 87, 100, 119, 177
FICO Score.. 36, 166, 168
Financial Habits...150, 168
Financial Planner 35, 152, 153, 169, 177
Fixer-Upper.. 68, 69
Floor Plan... 83, 90, 169
Fourplex 65
Free & Clear...169
Front End Ratio 41, 169
FSBO.. 60, 69, 177

GFE 56, 177
Good Money Management 151, 168, 169
GRI 28, 177
HERS 74, 177
HOA 16, 34, 41, 56, 57, 63, 66, 67, 77, 92, 103, 104, 124, 125, 148, 149, 163, 169, 177
Home Inspection 32, 45, 83, 89, 93, 94, 96, 101, 102, 112, 113, 116, 117, 119, 120, 121, 134, 158, 169
Home Warranty 85, 92, 93, 95, 96, 101, 147, 148, 159, 166, 169
Homeowner .. 13, 14, 16, 17, 18, 27, 32, 34, 44, 45, 54, 57, 81, 139, 142, 145, 148, 152, 158, 160, 163, 165, 166, 169, 170, 172
Homeowners Insurance 57, 104, 126, 127, 149, 168, 169, 170
HUD 44, 60, 66, 178
HUD-1 .... 103, 104, 105, 106, 128, 135, 159, 168, 178
Impound Account 168, 170
Instant Email Alerts 29, 61, 170
Insurance Policy.. 128, 170
Interest.. 31
InterNACHI 93, 178
Itemized Deductions 57, 170
Legacy..18, 129, 147, 155, 157, 170, 213
Legal Obligation 60, 170
Legal Service Plan 153, 170
Life Insurance 126, 152, 170
Life Span 146, 170
List Price 90, 91, 170, 174, 176
Living Trust 152, 153, 154, 171
LOE 128, 133, 178
Manufactured Home 66
Mello-Roos Fees 57, 171
MLS....................................... 29, 49, 61, 77, 79, 87, 178
Mobile Home 66
Mortgage Insurance... 57, 171, 178
Mortgage Loan...17, 18, 26, 32, 36, 37, 55, 103, 104, 128, 129, 133, 135, 136, 138, 159, 163, 166, 171, 177, 178
Move-Up Home 171
Mutual Agreement 102, 108, 171, 175
NACA... 76, 178
NAHI 93, 178
Negotiable 87, 91, 92, 95, 101, 102, 104, 105, 171
Negotiation Process 109, 111, 114, 171
Neighborhood Blight..171
Nest Egg 152, 171
New Home Builder 70
New Home Developer 96
Non-Traditional Construction 70
Notary Public 103, 105, 136, 137, 143, 171
NSF... 42, 178
Offer to Purchase 58, 75, 76, 77, 79, 82, 90, 91, 92, 171
Overlap Occupancy 130, 172
Owner-Occupant Buyers 172
P&L 54, 178
Personal Property...79, 86, 87, 101, 134, 172
Pest Control Inspection 92, 101, 102, 103, 172

PITI 57, 178
Plan B 52, 83, 111, 164
Planned Unit Development 56, 172, 178
PMI 41, 57, 169, 171, 178
POC 103, 178
POF 71, 76, 178
Preliminary Title Report 125, 172
Pre-Payment Penalty 172
Pre-Qualification Letter 48, 159, 172
Preventive Maintenance 46, 146, 173
Price Range 48, 61, 78, 81, 82, 90, 173
Principal 31, 38, 57, 104, 149, 173
Property Profile 92
Property Taxes 15, 104, 149, 168, 169, 170, 173
PUD 56, 63, 172, 178
Purchase Contract .17, 86, 92, 99, 100, 101, 103, 107, 113, 114, 123, 124, 132, 165, 173, 175
Qualification Letter 172, 173
Qualified 13, 17, 51, 54, 55, 58, 172, 173
Ratified Contract 173
REALTOR 13, 17, 26, 27, 28, 29, 48, 49, 51, 59, 60, 61, 62, 71, 72, 74, 75, 76, 77, 79, 80, 81, 83, 84, 85, 86, 88, 89, 90, 91, 92, 93, 94, 95, 97, 100, 102, 106, 108, 109, 110, 111, 112, 113, 114, 115, 117, 118, 119, 120, 121, 122, 123, 124, 125, 127, 130, 134, 135, 138, 140, 143, 144, 158, 160, 173, 177
Recorded Deed 173
REO 60, 69, 87, 88, 89, 102, 119, 173, 178
Repair Request 94, 112, 121, 134, 173
Row Homes 64
RPA 92, 99, 101, 178
Rural Property 69
Search Criteria 48, 61, 72, 174
Seasoned Funds 174
Service Call 96, 148, 174
Settlement Period 165
SFR 21, 62, 174, 178
Short Sale 55, 87, 88, 89, 92, 102, 118, 119, 129, 174
SI form 125, 178
Single Family Residence 174, 178
Special Assessments 124, 149, 174
Standard Forms 113, 114, 174
Starter Home 83, 174
Structural Condition 93, 175
Subject To 165, 175
Table Funding 137, 175
Tax Deductions 175
Tax-Deductible.. 114, 175
Termite Inspection 95
Title Company 88, 89, 102, 119, 125, 168, 175, 178
Title Insurance 45, 92, 102, 104, 105, 124, 125, 175
Title Report 124
Townhouses 64
Triplex 65
Twin Home 65, 175

Under Contract... 118, 164, 175
Underwriting 58, 104, 128, 173, 175, 177
USDA...52, 76, 87, 100, 119, 178
VA 52, 56, 64, 76, 87, 95, 100, 119, 164, 178
Valuation 90, 122, 176
Values .... i, 28, 151, 176, 213
Vesting 125, 159, 175
VP 135, 179
Walk-Through Inspection 176
Will 28, 153, 176
Wire... 131, 138, 176
Wish List 76, 78, 81, 82, 158, 160, 176
Zero-Down Loan...32, 41, 76, 176

FORMS

- Wish List
- Budget
- Loan Comparison
- Rent vs. Own Calculation
- Agent Interview
- House Comparison Form
- Vendors on your Team
- Offer Checklist

Wish List

Our Home Wish List

Buyer Name: _____   Date(s) of Search: _____

	MUST HAVE	WANT TO HAVE	CANNOT HAVE
House Characteristics:			
Bedrooms			
Bathrooms			
Family room			
Office / den			
Formal dining room			
Kitchen type (L, U, island, galley)			
Garage			
Fireplace			
Flooring			
Back yard			
Special features			
Location Criteria:			
Location (city, zip, neighborhood)			
Downtown / Suburban / Rural			
Proximity to work / school / church / recreation / shopping			
Miscellaneous Details:			
Age of home			
Street / Corner / Cul-de-sac			
Attached or Detached?			
Single level or Multi level?			
Walkability			
Traffic / Noise			
Amenities:			
Swimming Pool			
Other:			
Other:			
Other:			
Other:			

Wish List.docx   Printed 11/18/2012   Page 1 of 1
                                   copyright © HousePro Academy 2012

Budget Sample

Monthly Budget 2012 for the Sample Family

	Day/Month	January Projected	February Projected	March Projected	April Projected	May Projected	June Projected	July Projected	August Projected	September Projected	October Projected	November Projected	December Projected	TOTAL YEAR Projected
INCOME (Net)														
ABC Company	1st & 15th	$2,580.00	$2,580.00	$2,580.00	$2,580.00	$2,580.00	$2,580.00	$2,580.00	$2,580.00	$2,580.00	$2,580.00	$2,580.00	$2,580.00	$30,960.00
XYZ Corporation	Every FRI	$1,840.00	$1,840.00	$1,840.00	$1,840.00	$1,840.00	$1,840.00	$1,840.00	$1,840.00	$1,840.00	$1,840.00	$1,840.00	$1,840.00	$22,080.00
MLM self-employment	varies	$370.00	$370.00	$370.00	$370.00	$370.00	$370.00	$370.00	$370.00	$370.00	$370.00	$370.00	$370.00	$4,440.00
Book Royalties	30th	$55.00	$55.00	$55.00	$55.00	$55.00	$55.00	$55.00	$55.00	$55.00	$55.00	$55.00	$55.00	$660.00
TOTAL		$4,845.00	$4,845.00	$4,845.00	$4,845.00	$4,845.00	$4,845.00	$4,845.00	$4,845.00	$4,845.00	$4,845.00	$4,845.00	$4,845.00	$58,140.00
EXPENSES														
Housing:														
Rent / Mortgage	1st	$1,200.00	$1,200.00	$1,200.00	$1,200.00	$1,200.00	$1,200.00	$1,200.00	$1,200.00	$1,200.00	$1,200.00	$1,200.00	$1,200.00	$14,400.00
Home Maintenance	varies	$100.00	$100.00	$100.00	$100.00	$100.00	$100.00	$100.00	$100.00	$100.00	$100.00	$100.00	$100.00	$1,200.00
House Insurance	Jan/Jul	$50.00	$50.00	$50.00	$50.00	$50.00	$50.00	$50.00	$50.00	$50.00	$50.00	$50.00	$50.00	$600.00
House Taxes	Dec/Apr	$150.00	$150.00	$150.00	$150.00	$150.00	$150.00	$150.00	$150.00	$150.00	$150.00	$150.00	$150.00	$1,800.00
Automobile:														
Chevy	7th	$130.00	$130.00	$130.00	$130.00	$130.00	$130.00	$130.00	$130.00	$130.00	$130.00	$130.00	$130.00	$1,560.00
Dodge	19th	$210.00	$210.00	$210.00	$210.00	$210.00	$210.00	$210.00	$210.00	$210.00	$210.00	$210.00	$210.00	$2,520.00
Car Insurance	Jan/Jul	$100.00	$100.00	$100.00	$100.00	$100.00	$100.00	$100.00	$100.00	$100.00	$100.00	$100.00	$100.00	$1,200.00
Gasoline	varies	$100.00	$100.00	$100.00	$100.00	$100.00	$100.00	$100.00	$100.00	$100.00	$100.00	$100.00	$100.00	$1,200.00
Maintenance	varies	$50.00	$50.00	$50.00	$50.00	$50.00	$50.00	$50.00	$50.00	$50.00	$50.00	$50.00	$50.00	$600.00
Health/Medical:														
Health Insurance	2nd	$145.00	$145.00	$145.00	$145.00	$145.00	$145.00	$145.00	$145.00	$145.00	$145.00	$145.00	$145.00	$1,740.00
Medical/Dental Expenses	varies	$35.00	$35.00	$35.00	$35.00	$35.00	$35.00	$35.00	$35.00	$35.00	$35.00	$35.00	$35.00	$420.00
Utilities:														
Phone - regular	n/a	$0.00	$0.00	$0.00	$0.00	$0.00	$0.00	$0.00	$0.00	$0.00	$0.00	$0.00	$0.00	$0.00
Phone - long distance	n/a	$0.00	$0.00	$0.00	$0.00	$0.00	$0.00	$0.00	$0.00	$0.00	$0.00	$0.00	$0.00	$0.00
Phone - cell	12th	$200.00	$200.00	$200.00	$200.00	$200.00	$200.00	$200.00	$200.00	$200.00	$200.00	$200.00	$200.00	$2,400.00
PG&E (Electric)	18th	$110.00	$110.00	$110.00	$110.00	$110.00	$110.00	$110.00	$110.00	$110.00	$110.00	$110.00	$110.00	$1,320.00
Gas Co.	4th	$90.00	$90.00	$90.00	$90.00	$90.00	$90.00	$90.00	$90.00	$90.00	$90.00	$90.00	$90.00	$1,080.00
Water & Sewer	1st	$75.00	$75.00	$75.00	$75.00	$75.00	$75.00	$75.00	$75.00	$75.00	$75.00	$75.00	$75.00	$900.00
Trash	1st	$15.00	$15.00	$15.00	$15.00	$15.00	$15.00	$15.00	$15.00	$15.00	$15.00	$15.00	$15.00	$180.00
Cable	5th	$0.00	$0.00	$0.00	$0.00	$0.00	$0.00	$0.00	$0.00	$0.00	$0.00	$0.00	$0.00	$0.00
Food:														
Groceries	varies	$385.00	$385.00	$385.00	$385.00	$385.00	$385.00	$385.00	$385.00	$385.00	$385.00	$385.00	$385.00	$4,620.00
Dining Out	varies	$75.00	$75.00	$75.00	$75.00	$75.00	$75.00	$75.00	$75.00	$75.00	$75.00	$75.00	$75.00	$900.00
Education:														
Child Care	FRI	$50.00	$50.00	$50.00	$50.00	$50.00	$50.00	$50.00	$50.00	$50.00	$50.00	$50.00	$50.00	$600.00
Tuition & Books	n/a	$0.00	$0.00	$0.00	$0.00	$0.00	$0.00	$0.00	$0.00	$0.00	$0.00	$0.00	$0.00	$0.00
Continuing Education	varies	$40.00	$40.00	$40.00	$40.00	$40.00	$40.00	$40.00	$40.00	$40.00	$40.00	$40.00	$40.00	$480.00
Miscellaneous:														
Tithes (10% of income)	SUN	$484.50	$484.50	$484.50	$484.50	$484.50	$484.50	$484.50	$484.50	$484.50	$484.50	$484.50	$484.50	$5,814.00
Taxes	April	$40.00	$40.00	$40.00	$40.00	$40.00	$40.00	$40.00	$40.00	$40.00	$40.00	$40.00	$40.00	$480.00
Clothing	varies	$100.00	$100.00	$100.00	$100.00	$100.00	$100.00	$100.00	$100.00	$100.00	$100.00	$100.00	$100.00	$1,200.00
Entertainment	varies	$35.00	$35.00	$35.00	$35.00	$35.00	$35.00	$35.00	$35.00	$35.00	$35.00	$35.00	$35.00	$420.00
Sports / Dance (Kids)	1st	$70.00	$70.00	$70.00	$70.00	$70.00	$70.00	$70.00	$70.00	$70.00	$70.00	$70.00	$70.00	$840.00
Furniture	varies	$50.00	$50.00	$50.00	$50.00	$50.00	$50.00	$50.00	$50.00	$50.00	$50.00	$50.00	$50.00	$600.00
Electronics	varies	$40.00	$40.00	$40.00	$40.00	$40.00	$40.00	$40.00	$40.00	$40.00	$40.00	$40.00	$40.00	$480.00
Savings:														
Short Term Savings	1st & 15th	$100.00	$100.00	$100.00	$100.00	$100.00	$100.00	$100.00	$100.00	$100.00	$100.00	$100.00	$100.00	$1,200.00
Long Term Savings	15th	$50.00	$50.00	$50.00	$50.00	$50.00	$50.00	$50.00	$50.00	$50.00	$50.00	$50.00	$50.00	$600.00
Investments	15th	$50.00	$50.00	$50.00	$50.00	$50.00	$50.00	$50.00	$50.00	$50.00	$50.00	$50.00	$50.00	$600.00
Christmas Savings	15th	$50.00	$50.00	$50.00	$50.00	$50.00	$50.00	$50.00	$50.00	$50.00	$50.00	$50.00	$50.00	$600.00
Debt payoff:														
Department Store Credit	7th	$25.00	$25.00	$25.00	$25.00	$25.00	$25.00	$25.00	$25.00	$25.00	$25.00	$25.00	$25.00	$300.00
Student Loan	1st	$100.00	$100.00	$100.00	$100.00	$100.00	$100.00	$100.00	$100.00	$100.00	$100.00	$100.00	$100.00	$1,200.00
Loan from parents	15th	$50.00	$50.00	$50.00	$50.00	$50.00	$50.00	$50.00	$50.00	$50.00	$50.00	$50.00	$50.00	$600.00
Other:														
Donations	varies	$45.00	$45.00	$45.00	$45.00	$45.00	$45.00	$45.00	$45.00	$45.00	$45.00	$45.00	$45.00	$540.00
Christmas/Other Gifts	varies	$50.00	$50.00	$50.00	$50.00	$50.00	$50.00	$50.00	$50.00	$50.00	$50.00	$50.00	$50.00	$99.00
Miscellaneous	varies	$30.00	$30.00	$30.00	$30.00	$30.00	$30.00	$30.00	$30.00	$30.00	$30.00	$30.00	$30.00	$360.00
TOTAL		$4,679.50	$4,679.50	$4,679.50	$4,679.50	$4,679.50	$4,679.50	$4,679.50	$4,679.50	$4,679.50	$4,679.50	$4,679.50	$4,679.50	$55,653.00
MONTHLY CASH FLOW		$165.50	$165.50	$165.50	$165.50	$165.50	$165.50	$165.50	$165.50	$165.50	$165.50	$165.50	$165.50	$2,487.00

Budget Blank, Page 1

Monthly Budget 2012

INCOME

	Job #1	Job #2	Job #3	Financial Aid	Gift	Other	Other	TOTAL

EXPENSES

Housing:
- Rent / Mortgage
- Home Maintenance
- House Insurance
- House Taxes

Automobile:
- Car Payment #1
- Car Payment #2
- Car Insurance
- Gasoline
- Maintenance

Health/Medical:
- Health Insurance
- Medical/Dental Expenses

Utilities:
- Phone - regular
- Phone - long distance
- Phone - cell
- PG&E (Electric)
- Gas Co.
- Water & Sewer
- Trash
- Cable

Food:
- Groceries
- Dining Out

Education:
- Tuition & Books
- Continuing Education

Miscellaneous:
- Tithes
- Taxes
- Clothing
- Entertainment
- Classes
- Furniture
- Electronics

Savings:
- Short Term Savings
- Long Term Savings
- Investments
- Christmas Savings

Debt payoff:
- Credit Card #1
- Credit Card #2
- Loan #1
- Loan #2
- Other _____
- Other _____

Other:
- Donations
- Christmas/Other Gifts
- Other

TOTAL

MONTHLY CASH FLOW

(Columns: DayMonth | Projected | Actual | Difference for each of the months January, February, March, April, May, June. All value cells contain $0.00.)

Budget Blank, Page 2

Monthly Budget

	July			August			September			October			November			December			TOTAL YEAR		
	Projected	Actual	Difference	Projected	Actual	Difference	Projected	Actual	Difference	Projected	Actual	Difference	Projected	Actual	Difference	Projected	Actual	Difference	Projected	Actual	Difference

Loan Comparison

Mortgage Loan Comparison

Loan Scenario Details

Buyer Names: _____   Lender: _____

	Loan #1	Loan #2	Loan #3
Loan Type (FHA, VA, conventional)			
Maximum loan amount $			
Downpayment %			
Downpayment $			
Interest Rate %			
Fixed or Adjustable?			
Monthly Payments (principal & interest) $			
PMI (Mortgage Insurance) required?			
APR Rate %			
# of Years			
Points			
Other Fees			
Prepayment penalty?			
Interest rate cap			
Type of index			
Interest rate adjustments			
Assumable?			
Allow downpayment assistance?			
Closing timeframe (# of days to fund)			
Condo complex needs to be approved?			

Notes: _____

_____

_____

Rent vs. Own Calculation

Rent vs. Own Calculation

Property Address: _____

RENT		
	Current Rent:	$0.00
	Parking Fees:	$0.00
	Other Housing Expenses:	$0.00
	Total Rent:	$0.00

OWN		
	Mortgage Payment:	$0.00
	Taxes*:	$0.00
	Insurance*:	$0.00
	Mortgage Insurance:	$0.00
	HOA fees:	$0.00
	Other:	$0.00
	Total Own:	$0.00

*Calculate annual amount due divided by 12 months to equal monthly payment

Loan Summary:

Type:	
Purchase Price:	
Interest Rate:	
Years Amortized:	
Down Payment:	

Agent Interview

Real Estate Agent Interview

Buyer Names: _____   Date: _____

Agent Name: _____   Company: _____

Questions for Discussion

1. What's your background? (education & experience) _____
2. When did you get your real estate license? _____
3. What designations or certifications have you achieved? _____
4. How often do you take courses for professional development? _____
5. Are you a Realtor® member? _____
6. What geographic area do you serve? _____
7. What MLS's do you belong to? _____
8. Do you attend your local MLS meeting weekly? _____
9. Do you participate in your Realtor® caravan & preview new listings weekly? _____
10. How many first home buyers have you represented? _____
11. Who is your preferred mortgage lender? _____
12. Who do you recommend as a home inspector? _____
13. What is your preferred communication type? (email, phone, text) _____
14. What days/times you are available? _____
15. How often do you update your buyers? _____
16. What is your experience in negotiating for your buyers? _____
17. What do you expect from your buyer clients? _____
18. What do you like best about your job? _____
19. What do you like least about your job? _____
20. What fees will we owe you for representing us? _____
21. What do you do better than anyone else? _____
22. Why should we hire you? _____
23. Please send us your Capabilities Statement or resume. _____

Notes: _____

_____

Hired: ❏ YES   ❏ NO   Date Hired: _____

Agent Interview.docx   Printed 11/18/2012   Page 1 of 1
                    copyright © HousePro Academy 2012

House Comparison Form

House Search Comparison Form

Buyer Name: _____ Date(s) of Search: _____

	Ideal	Property #1	Property #2	Property #3
Street Address	---			
Asking Price				
City				
Bedrooms				
Bathrooms				
Living Room				
Kitchen				
Dining Area				
Family Room				
Den / Office				
Garage				
Front Yard				
Back Yard				
Porch / Patio				
Carpet				
Vinyl / Tile				
Paint Inside				
Paint Outside				
Roof Condition				
Storage Areas				
Fences				
Water Heater				
Neighborhood				
Other				

Notes: _____

_____

_____

House Search Comparison Form - PAGE 2

Buyer Name: _____   Date(s) of Search: _____

	Property #4	Property #5	Property #6	Property #7
Street Address				
Asking Price				
City				
Bedrooms				
Bathrooms				
Living Room				
Kitchen				
Dining Area				
Family Room				
Den / Office				
Garage				
Front Yard				
Back Yard				
Porch / Patio				
Carpet				
Vinyl / Tile				
Paint Inside				
Paint Outside				
Roof Condition				
Storage Areas				
Fences				
Water Heater				
Neighborhood				
Other				

Notes: _____

_____

House Search Comparison Form - PAGE 3

Buyer Name: _____ Date(s) of Search: _____

	Property #8	Property #9	Property #10	Property #11
Street Address				
Asking Price				
City				
Bedrooms				
Bathrooms				
Living Room				
Kitchen				
Dining Area				
Family Room				
Den / Office				
Garage				
Front Yard				
Back Yard				
Porch / Patio				
Carpet				
Vinyl / Tile				
Paint Inside				
Paint Outside				
Roof Condition				
Storage Areas				
Fences				
Water Heater				
Neighborhood				
Other				

Notes: _____

_____

House Comparison.docx   Printed 11/18/2012   *Page 3 of 4*
copyright © HousePro Academy 2012

House Ratings

	Home Address	Ranking (1-10 scale)	Comments
1			
2			
3			
4			
5			
6			
7			
8			
9			
10			
11			

House Comparison

Top Rating	House #	Comments
#1		
#2		
#3		
#4		
#5		
#6		
#7		
#8		
#9		
#10		

Notes: _____

_____

_____

_____

_____

_____

_____

Vendors on Your Team

Vendors on your Team

HANDY REFERENCE LIST

Buyer Name: _____   Date: _____

Vendor	Name	Phone	Email
Realtor®			
Mortgage Lender			
Home Inspector			
Termite Inspector			
Escrow/Settlement Officer			
Title Insurance Rep			
Insurance Agent			
Financial Advisor			
Attorney			
Tax Preparer			
Other:			
Other:			
Other:			

Vendors Team.docx   Printed 11/18/2012   Page 1 of 1
copyright © HousePro Academy 2012

Offer Checklist

Offer Checklist & Summary

Buyer Names: _____   Agent: _____

Property Address: _____   Date of Offer: _____

Offer Details:

Purchase Price Amount:	
Earnest Money Deposit:	
Total Downpayment:	
Concessions / Credits:	
Closing Date:	
Escrow/Settlement Company:	
Title Insurance Company:	
Appliances Included:	
Home Warranty paid by whom?	
Short Sale or REO?	
Other:	
Counter Offer #1	
Counter Offer #2	

Reports/Inspections:

Report Type	Date Received
Physical Home Inspection	
Pest Control Inspection	
Appraisal	
HOA info	
Other:	

Important Dates to Track

Item	Date Due
Request for Repairs	
Contingency Removal	
HUD-1 Approved	
Appraisal	
Loan Funding	
Closing Date	
Other:	

Notes: _____

_____

_____

Offer Checklist.doc   Printed 11/18/2012   Page 1 of 1
copyright © HousePro Academy 2012

ABOUT US

- About HousePro Academy
- Author Biography

About HousePro Academy

Let's get you and your family started on that all-important path toward home ownership. Do not take our country's great values for granted. Your opportunity for homeownership is available to you, so take advantage of it today! We at HousePro Academy will be here every step of the way.

You may be asking, "Just what is HousePro Academy?" Well, we are a specially formed online training course and certification academy. Our goal is to help Americans achieve a better financial future, and by working together, we will improve our economy. We offer many courses here at HousePro Academy for consumer education, protection, and achievement. We are social, financial, and environmental advocates for you, the consumer.

Homebuyers and House Sellers

We offer courses to homebuyers and sellers throughout the United States and North America. Our goal is for every American family to be able to own their own home. By teaching renters how to get qualified and purchase a house, we will all have more stable and secure neighborhoods. We strongly believe that home ownership is the key to healthy, thriving cities and communities.

Home Ownership Maintenance

Once you purchase your home, what is next? We show you how to maintain your home through our "Home Ownership Maintenance" course. This online workshop is coming soon, so please stay tuned.

Financial Stewardship

We also offer financial stewardship courses to help you better understand and manage your money, so that you can leave a lasting legacy for your family. We know that home ownership is the foundation and cornerstone of a good economic plan. We want you to start on the right path, and we will notify you when this online workshop is ready.

Hands-on Workshops

We offer hands-on training workshops throughout the States, and especially in California. Our popular "Lunch and Learn" workshops are requested by employers. We also offer homebuyer courses in the evenings and on weekends to accommodate the schedule of homebuyers like you. Since our time is limited and we cannot travel all across the United States to meet you in person, we have come up with a great solution: *offer online training courses*.

Author Biography

Regina P. Brown is a California Real Estate Broker, licensed since 1988. Her passion is helping families create their legacy through financial education. She offers real estate seminars and consults extensively with clients one-on-one. Because she has experienced 2 full real estate economic cycles, she has learned how to successfully solve many challenging situations.

Ms. Brown is a strong advocate for families, consumers, and her clients. Her mission is to:

- Raise the bar for real estate and mortgage industry professionals
- Educate consumers, be an advocate, and help bring positive change to our economic system
- Assist families to increase their financial knowledge, economic independence, and wealth freedom through individual counseling and published resources

My passion is to help Americans become financially stable. I believe that homeownership is a critical cornerstone of their financial plan for the future. To get this important message out to the millions of families, we decided the most effective method to reach prospective home buyers would be a book!

Yes, you too can become a homeowner. Follow us as we show you how to navigate the home buying process with success!

Educated with degrees in Real Estate and Small Business Management, she is also prepared with a Technical Writing Certificate. Ms. Brown uses her skills to advise her clients and actively contributes her time to the community and professional associations. Her professional experience and community involvement includes: REALTOR® Association committee member, ePro REALTOR® certification, GREEN real estate agent certification, *Habitat for Humanity* board member, Junior Achievement volunteer, and Sunday School teacher at her local Christian church.

Ms. Brown attends continuing education classes and stays abreast of the ever-changing real estate industry. She looks forward to helping shape the future of the real estate industry and American family economics.